The Light of Learning

The Light
of Learning

SELECTED WRITINGS ON
EDUCATION

DAISAKU
IKEDA

MIDDLEWAY
PRESS

Published by Middleway Press
A division of the SGI-USA
606 Wilshire Blvd., Santa Monica, CA 90401

Cover and interior design by Gopa & Ted2, Inc.

25 24 23 22 21   1 2 3 4 5

ISBN: 978-0-9723267-3-5

Library of Congress Cataloging-in-Publication Data:
Names: Ikeda, Daisaku, author.
Title: The light of learning : Daisaku Ikeda on education / Daisaku Ikeda.
Description: Santa Monica, CA : Middleway Press, [2021] | Includes index. |
   Summary: "A new selection of writings on education by Buddhist
   philosopher and founder of Soka University, Daisaku Ikeda. Culled from
   some five decades of the author's works, this collection presents
   educational proposals, lectures to university students, and personal
   essays. The author delves not only into the meaning of *soka*
   (value-creating) education but offers a hopeful vision of the power of
   education to bring happiness to the individual and peace to the world."
   — Provided by publisher.
Identifiers: LCCN 2021030159 (print) | LCCN 2021030160 (ebook) |
   ISBN 9780972326735 | ISBN 9781946635648 (ebook)
Subjects: LCSH: Education–Philosophy. | Sōka Gakkai.
Classification: LCC LB880 .I36 2021 (print) | LCC LB880 (ebook) |
   DDC 370.1–dc23
LC record available at https://lccn.loc.gov/2021030159
LC ebook record available at https://lccn.loc.gov/2021030160

Contents

Foreword

THIS ENDURING VOLUME—published here in its third edition with a new title, six new works, and revised translations—introduces readers to the educational philosophy and practice of Daisaku Ikeda. Known widely as a global peacebuilder and president of the lay Buddhist organization Soka Gakkai International, Ikeda has also distinguished himself as an important educator on the world stage. From his first publication, written at age twenty-one,[1] to the Soka schools, universities, and women's college that he has founded across Asia and the Americas, Ikeda has for more than seven decades advanced education and lifelong learning as the surest means of truly human becoming, peaceful coexistence, and genuine happiness for oneself and others.

The writings in this edited collection, which constitute only a portion of Ikeda's entire corpus on education, span multiple decades and represent many of the diverse voices, modes, and styles characteristic of his oeuvre—poetry, energetic and personal prose, essays, speeches, and detailed proposals. They address two audiences he regularly seeks to encourage and support with his educational approaches, perspectives, and convictions. One of these audiences, as seen in five of the newly included writings, is the students, faculty, and staff at the Soka institutions and organizations he has established, including the many members of the Soka Gakkai Educators

Division in Japan. The other is the entire field of education broadly conceived—from teacher educators and university scholars across diverse disciplines to teachers, leaders, and counselors in pre-K–12 schools around the world; from policymakers and advocates to practitioners of home- and community-based learning in multicultural, multiracial, and multilingual contexts.

A distinguishing feature of this collection is not only that it assembles these works in one volume but that, in doing so, it presents a comprehensive view of Ikeda as both a practitioner and philosopher. That is, while Ikeda is not a classroom teacher or administrator, we see in these writings his characteristic manner of encouraging, appreciating, and directly engaging in life-to-life exchanges with students and those responsible for fostering and teaching them. We also see a careful thinker addressing the most pressing and timeless issues in education: from peace and human rights to the cultivation of our humanity and creativity; from ecological sustainability to the deepening of our appreciation for great works of literature; from the profound significance of dialogue and inner transformation to the removal of education from politicization and the ever-changing whimsy of government authority, among many others. In all, Ikeda advances an approach to education that is clear eyed and aspirational, practical and philosophical, uniquely Eastern and quintessentially universal. It is an approach radiant with the belief that each of us matters and all of us possess the infinite potential to develop in our own humanity and pioneer a better age.

Human Education

Ikeda calls his approach *ningen kyoiku* (人間教育), or "human education." On one hand, this approach is shaped by his faith in the Lotus Sutra–centric teachings of the thirteenth-century Buddhist reformer Nichiren (1222–82) and is a secular manifestation of it. For Ikeda, "human education and Buddhism are two aspects of the same reality."[2] Both seek to enhance our humanity. In other words, if the purpose of Buddhism is to alleviate the sufferings of life for oneself and others, so it must be for education. And if the purpose of Buddhism is for us to awaken to the preciousness, dignity, true nature, and unlimited potential of one's own life and that of others, so it must be for education. As Ikeda puts it, "Being born human does not make one a human being. Don't we really only become human when we make tenacious effort to live as human beings? . . . That's why education is so important. We need human education to become human beings."[3]

While Ikeda regularly crosses conceptual and semantic boundaries between the religious and the mundane, bringing insights and terminology from Buddhism to secular affairs and identifying examples from the secular world to illuminate Buddhist principles, this does not mean that he advocates for proselytizing or teaching Buddhism in schools. As he states in multiple writings in this volume, he explicitly opposes that, having experienced the consequences of compulsory religious education preceding and during World War II. Rather, he advocates for the "need to cultivate a sense of belonging to humanity as a whole"[4] and emphasizes a human-centered spirituality, interdependent totality, and characteristics that will enable individuals to enjoy personal growth and contribute to society.[5]

In concrete terms, human education is twofold. It is an
approach that calls on us to encourage the individual right
in front of us, to believe in everyone's unique and unlimited
potential, including one's own, and to never give up on anyone, no matter what. But it also, equally, demands that we
awaken to the full scope and possibility of our own humanity and human-ness. For Ikeda, being human is an action, a
continual process of *being* and *becoming* more "fully human"
through persistent dialogic engagement with the "profoundly
internalized 'other'" in all its forms.[6] Whether with nature,
cultures, entire civilizations or strangers, family, friends, or
any manner of teacher in our surroundings, such dialogue
encourages us to see the other in ourselves, ourselves in the
other, and to perceive a deeper mutuality and connection.
Thus Ikeda calls for a shift, in both perspective and practice,
from *education*, pronounced *kyoiku* in Japanese and written
with a character compound (教育) that suggests a primacy
on one-directional "teaching," to the homophone *kyoiku*, or
mutual fostering, written instead with characters (共育) that prioritize "mutual growth" born from a two-way vector of influence between self and other, teacher and taught.[7] As he states,

> The individual growth of a single person will inspire
> the growth of others and, further, will encourage
> the growth of one's community and society—this is
> precisely the principle of a great human revolution.
> Therefore, if the teacher grows, children will as a mat-
> ter of course grow. Moreover, for teachers to grow,
> they must learn from the students' growth. Education
> [*kyoiku*; 教育] is *mutual growth* [*kyoiku*; 共育] born from
> the teacher and student developing together and fos-
> tering one another.[8]

The Heritage of Makiguchi and Toda

Ikeda's approach of human education is also informed by his commitment to the thought and convictions of Tsunesaburo Makiguchi (1871–1944) and Josei Toda (1900–58). Ikeda did not know Makiguchi personally but came to know of him and his work through his close, decade-long tutelage under Toda. Toda's influence on Ikeda cannot be overstated and forms the core of his perspective on the deeply transformational effect a heart-to-heart, life-to-life relationship between teacher and taught can have on both. Ninety-eight percent of what Ikeda is, he asserts, he learned from Toda.

Makiguchi was an elementary school teacher and principal whose penetrating scholarship spanned areas such as reading and writing, human geography, communities studies, and perhaps most significant, questions of value. He introduced his theory of value and value-creating pedagogy in the four-volume work *Soka kyoikugaku taikei* (The System of Value-Creating Pedagogy).

Drawing on decades of his own classroom practice, Makiguchi distinguished truth from value, seeking to clarify the often-confused psychological processes of cognition (understanding something as it objectively is) and evaluation (determining its relevance to life). Facticity alone does not make truth meaningful to our lives, he argued. Rather, the significance of truth in our lives comes from the subjective and contingent value or meaning we create from it. Therefore, Makiguchi advocated for a pedagogical practice that helps learners create value in terms of gain, good, and beauty—that is, aesthetically pleasing and utilitarian value that serves oneself and others. Moreover, he asserted that such value creation is what demonstrates agency and cultivates genuine, almost

existential happiness. Toda was a close colleague of Makiguchi and applied value-creating approaches to great success in
his Jishu Gakkan, a tutorial school he founded.

Coinciding with *The Pedagogy's* release, Makiguchi and Toda
also established the Soka Kyoiku Gakkai (Value-Creating Education Society), the forerunner to the Soka Gakkai and Soka
Gakkai International. The Soka Kyoiku Gakkai originally
comprised a group of reform-minded educators with a diverse
range of motivations, including a generic dissatisfaction felt
by all teachers who believe they could be doing better for
their students. They also shared a discontentment with Japan's
national education system and its escalating focus on cultivating subjects of an increasingly militarized state—a system that
would eventually include Ikeda among its first generation of
pupils. The group turned to Makiguchi's value-creating pedagogy as a viable alternative and developed a steadily growing
emphasis on Nichiren's teachings, to which Makiguchi and
Toda had converted in 1928, two years before they published
the first volume of *The Pedagogy*. The Soka Kyoiku Gakkai thus
sought to reform society through value-creating pedagogy in
schools, on the one hand, and through members' own faith-
based inner transformation, on the other.

Makiguchi and Toda were arrested and imprisoned for their
Buddhist-based opposition to the Japanese military authorities. Makiguchi died in prison, but Toda was released in 1945
and immediately worked to reestablish the group, broadening
its focus and renaming it Soka Gakkai. At age nineteen, Ikeda,
disillusioned in the aftermath of the war, attended a neighborhood lecture by Toda on "life philosophy." As he puts it:

> I suppose it's fair to say that nothing was quite as
> remote for a young person in the immediate postwar

period as talk of religion, particularly Buddhism. To tell the truth, I had no understanding at all of religion or Buddhism in those days. When I heard Mr. Toda's talk and saw him face to face, I made up my mind to walk the way of faith. Here, I thought, is a man I can follow.[9]

Ikeda succeeded Toda as president of Soka Gakkai in 1960 and expanded the organization worldwide, creating the Soka Gakkai International (SGI) in 1975. Today, the SGI claims affiliate members in 192 countries and territories. Ikeda built on the organization's foundations in education while also actively pursuing initiatives in peace and culture. In this sense, if Makiguchi introduced and enacted the pedagogical practice of creating value—or *soka*—at an individual level, and Toda applied it institution-wide in the Jishu Gakkan, then Ikeda must be recognized for distilling it into its crystalline essence, expanding this essence globally, and memorializing it as the foundational ethos and namesake of the schools and universities he founded. The practice of value creation thus endures as a constituent element of Ikeda's philosophy of human education and as a focus of SGI members under his leadership.[10]

The Light of Learning: A New Title and Revised Translations

Readers familiar with previous editions of this collection will immediately recognize its new title and updated translations. These important changes not only calibrate translations of key terms and concepts in the author's work, but they also provide a more accurate and articulate understanding of the scope of Ikeda's ideas.

In this regard, we must remember that Ikeda writes in Japanese and that his writings here were originally rendered into English by various translators across time. We must also remember that translation is not an exact science but a complex and skillful art that, in the best of circumstances, draws on bilingual proficiency and a studied knowledge of the intrinsic context of the original work. And it is *choice*. In some instances, words in translations are just ones the translator chose from an array of possibilities and may not necessarily convey a particular intention that readers might otherwise attribute to them based on their own sociocultural, political, or historical views and contexts.

In other instances, words matter. Authors use specific terms and concepts with intention. Moreover, translation adheres to *domestication* (bringing the writer to the reader) or *foreignization* (bringing the reader to the writer), with Ikeda's writings typically aligned to the former so they read as if originally written in English. Under this approach, unique terms and ideas that have no clear equivalents are rendered into the closest available, if imprecise, English terms rather than being transliterated or otherwise retaining their conceptual uniqueness and cultural "foreignness." Recognizing this practice is particularly important when translating from Japanese, a language whose high-context ideographic orthography can both compress and, more often, contain multiple meanings simultaneously within single words and character-compound phrases. The conventions of English, however, often require translators to choose a single meaning from among the many possible and leave the others unsaid.

All this pertains to the revised translations of four key terms pervading Ikeda's writings: *ningen kyoiku* (人間教育), *sekai*

shimin (世界市民), *kyosei* (共生), and *soka kyoiku* (創価教育). I
address each below.

Ikeda's term *ningen kyoiku* had been translated in past
editions as "humanistic education." It has been changed to
"human education" throughout. There are multiple reasons
for this. First, Ikeda's purposeful term differs from those often
used to translate "humanistic education" into Japanese: *nin-*
genshugi kyoiku (人間主義教育) and *ningenshugiteki kyoiku* (
人間主義的教育). Although Ikeda's approach certainly resonates in some ways with the lineage of humanistic education
from Jean-Jacques Rousseau (1712–78) and Johann Heinrich
Pestalozzi (1746–1827), conflating it with humanistic education, popularized in the 1960s through the 1980s and now
often dismissed as passé or Pollyannaish, would be incorrect
and a mischaracterization. Human education is the most apt
rendering for Ikeda's unique approach.

Second, the Eastern, Buddhist perspective that underpins
Ikeda's approach differs in important ways from Western,
Enlightenment notions of humanism that shape humanistic education and that are increasingly critiqued in the age
of climate change and embracing diversity in all its forms.
For example, advocates for a "posthumanist" philosophy
more expansive and inclusive than traditional humanism
challenge humanism for positioning human beings as fundamentally separate from nature, climate, and the nonhu-
man world, and for idealizing humankind in White, male,
elite, and heteronormative terms. On the contrary, Ikeda's
Buddhist perspective views humanity as inherently diverse,
complex, and irrevocably interdependent with all phenomena, including the biosphere. At the same time, human education exists in what Ikeda calls a "life-sized paradigm" by

which to understand the world and our place in it. By "life-sized" he means "a way of thinking that never deviates from the human scale. It is simultaneously a humane sensitivity to life as a whole and also to the details of everyday human existence."[11] Such a view allows us to experience our own growth and development relative to that of others and to the pressing global challenges of our age.

Sekai shimin. For decades, Ikeda has advanced the principle of global citizenship to confront many of life's pressing challenges, including racism, the clash of civilizations, and climate change.[12] He has used multiple Japanese terms to express this ethic, including most consistently *sekai shimin.* While this term literally means "world citizen" or "world citizenship," all instances herein have been translated as "global citizenship" to align with the standard English phrasing in the field.

Kyosei, literally "symbiosis" or "coexistence," is also a key term for Ikeda. It had been translated as "peaceful coexistence," "harmonious coexistence," and "creative coexistence." Creative coexistence, however, most comprehensively conveys Ikeda's usage because it captures his vision of interdependence as more than just a passive state of relationality. For him, relationality is—or can be—conscious, volitional, and based on *creativity* and *value creation.* In this sense, human beings must actively work at peaceful and harmonious coexistence by creating value for oneself and others in each moment and in every interaction with everyone and everything. Together with global citizenship, value creation, and dialogue, creative coexistence is one of four interlocking commitments and ideals of Ikeda's philosophy of human education.[13]

The last key term is *soka kyoiku,* or "value-creating education." Ikeda often uses this phrase relative to Makiguchi's pedagogy; that is, as a generic and concrete instructional practice possible by anyone anywhere. One could also read him using it as an implicit expression of an ethos passed down from Makiguchi and Toda that is inherent in the spirit and mission of the Soka institutions he founded. To convey this latter sense, translators of Ikeda's work have chosen to create the unique proper noun Soka Education (also Soka education). Japanese orthography does not differentiate proper from common nouns, but English conventions of capitalization and italicization to denote foreign words make the inherent difference explicit. That is, *soka* (italicized with a lower case *s*)[14] is a transliteration of the neologism referring to generic practices of "creating" (*sozo*) "value" (*kachi*) that are universally applicable in theory, research, and practice. Soka (unitalicized with a capital "S") is a proper name and connotes a kind of global "brand" or culture synonymous with the institutions and organizations Ikeda founded.

Middleway Press had adopted *Soka Education* as the title for previous editions of this collection; however, Ikeda does not label the majority of his particular ideas, concepts, and proposals with the term *soka kyoiku*, in either sense. Rather, value-creating education, the more prevalent use herein, is one important part of his comprehensive and far-reaching educational philosophy and practice. Writings in this volume have been revised accordingly and the title has been changed to *The Light of Learning*, which, like the titular poem that opens this collection, expresses Ikeda's broad vision that persistent learning across our lifespans is "incomparable proof / of human dignity / . . . our / proudest, most resounding / victory as humans, / our unique right and privilege."[15] Such human education is "the mission of every individual,"[16] the light in the darkness that can instantly spark hope and joy that brightens everything.

Concluding Thoughts

In the twenty years since this collection first appeared, Ikeda studies has emerged as a significant and growing discipline not only in education but also in the arts, literary commentary, religion, peace and human rights, citizen diplomacy, nuclear abolition, climate justice, and other areas. Engagement with his ideas and contributions has inspired conferences, symposia, and scholarly publications in Africa, Asia, Europe, and the Americas. In the field of education, academics are increasingly teaching and engaging with Ikeda's thought in theory and practice, and tens of universities around the world have established centers and initiatives to research his ideas. My own institution, DePaul University, the largest Catholic university and one of the largest private universities in the United States, established the first such center in the Anglophone academy in 2014 and offers degree and credential programs in Value-Creating Education for Global Citizenship based on Ikeda's work. To date, more than a thousand DePaul graduates—pre- and in-service educators—have studied Ikeda's ideas, and many are applying them to great success with all kinds of learners across diverse disciplines and contexts. They are not alone. Ikeda's perspectives similarly inform the practice of thousands of educators around the world.

The writings in this volume are compelling and encouraging, a necessary guide in the uncertainty of our turbulent times and the urgency of the moment. They will resonate with all readers, whether scholar or practitioner, initiated or new to Ikeda's work. Embodying his characteristic commitment to penetrating dialogue, they are ultimately an invitation to all of us to imagine possibility in the given, create value in our relationality, and to know others and ourselves and become truly human.

—Jason Goulah
Professor and Director
Institute for Daisaku Ikeda Studies, DePaul University

The Light of Learning

March 28, 2021

To learn is to offer
incomparable proof
of human dignity.
Learning is our
proudest, most resounding
victory as humans,
our unique right and privilege.
By learning,
we can bring forth the
magnificent capabilities
hidden in the depths
of our lives.
Through learning
we can fight for what is right
and help others
enjoy happiness.

When individuals,
societies, or civilizations
cease to learn,
they begin to decline.
This is the stark actuality
of history.

The path of consistent learning
will never be blocked.
A new and vital path
for the creation of value
will open without fail.

The purpose of learning
is to further
people's happiness.
It is to contribute
to the lives of
our fellow citizens.
It is to express our gratitude
to our parents.
It is to win the future.
A person who continues to learn
will never know defeat.

Always remember
that victory in life
will be determined by
our stance on learning,
whether we maintain
fresh and renewed vitality
as we ascend the slope of life,
today surpassing yesterday,
tomorrow surpassing today.
The true meaning of learning
is not limited to the acquisition
of new knowledge.
Rather, it is whether you,

through learning,
become a new you.

Never lose the desire
to learn and grow.
Continue to forge ahead.
The path on which you advance,
is yours and yours alone
and will become—
a path of mission,
a path of fulfillment,
a path of victory.

Timeline

July 1871[*]   Tsunesaburo Makiguchi born in Niigata
                       Prefecture, Japan.

February 1900   Josei Toda born in Ishikawa Prefecture,
                       Japan.

October 1903   Makiguchi publishes his first major work,
                       Jinsei chirigaku (The Geography of Human
                       Life).

April 1913   Makiguchi appointed principal of Tosei
                       Elementary School and its affiliated Shi-
                       taya Night School; he would serve as prin-
                       cipal of a series of elementary schools in
                       Tokyo until March 1932.

January 1920   Toda encounters Makiguchi and chooses
                       him as his mentor.

January 1928   Daisaku Ikeda born in Tokyo, Japan.

June 1930   Toda publishes *Suirishiki shido sanjutsu* (A
                       Deductive Guide to Arithmetic).

November 1930   Makiguchi and Toda publish *Soka kyoi-
                       kugaku taikei* (The System of Value-Creating
                       Pedagogy).

*June in the lunar calendar in use in Japan at the time.

July 1943	Makiguchi and Toda arrested and jailed by Japan's militarist government.
November 1944	Makiguchi dies in prison.
August 1947	Ikeda encounters Toda, deciding on Toda as his mentor.
April 1958	Toda dies.
April 1968	Soka Junior and Senior High Schools open in Tokyo.
April 1971	Soka University opens.
April 1973	Kansai Soka Junior and Senior High Schools open in Osaka.
April 1976	Sapporo Soka Kindergarten opens.
April 1978	Tokyo Soka Elementary School opens.
April 1982	Kansai Soka Elementary School opens.
April 1985	Soka Women's College opens.
September 1992	Hong Kong Soka Kindergarten opens. (To date, Soka Kindergartens have opened in Korea, Singapore, Malaysia, and Brazil.)
May 2001	Soka University of America opens in Aliso Viejo, California, as a four-year liberal arts college.
January 2017	Soka High School of Brazil opens.
February 2021	Announcement made that the Soka International School Malaysia will open in 2023.

part one:

addresses and proposals

Thoughts on Education for Global Citizenship

Teachers College, Columbia University, New York, June 13, 1996.

JUST AS THE CURRENTS of the Hudson River flow cease-lessly, with power and grandeur, Teachers College is pro-ducing an unbroken stream of youthful leaders who will create a magnificent new era in the coming century. It is an unparalleled honor to be able to speak here today at the pre-mier institute for graduate study in education in the United States, a monarch in the world of education, whose crown sends forth brilliant beams that light the future. I would like to offer my heartfelt gratitude to President Arthur E. Levine (1948—) and all those whose support has made this event a reality. I would also like to thank in advance our distinguished commentators who will later be sharing with us their enlight-ening views.

In 1975, it was my privilege to visit Columbia University. Four years earlier, in 1971, we had established Soka University in Tokyo. The warm encouragement and invaluable advice for a university still in its infancy, which we received at that time, is something that I will never forget. Thank you very much.

It is with profound emotion that I speak today at the col-lege where the world-renowned philosopher John Dewey (1859–1952) taught. The first president of the Soka Gakkai, Tsunesaburo Makiguchi (1871–1944), whose thinking is the founding spirit of Soka University, referenced with great respect the writings and ideas of Dewey in his 1930 work, *Soka kyoikugaku taikei* (The System of Value-Creating Pedagogy).

My own interest in and commitment to education stem from my experiences during World War II. My four elder brothers were drafted and sent to the front; the eldest was killed in action in Burma (present-day Myanmar). In the years immediately following the end of the war, my three surviving brothers returned one after another from the Chinese mainland. In their tattered uniforms, they were a truly pathetic sight. My parents were already aged; my father's pain, my mother's sadness were searing. To the end of my days, I will never forget the disgust and anger with which my eldest brother, on leave from China, had described the inhuman atrocities committed there by the Japanese army. I developed a deep hatred for war, its cruelty, stupidity, and waste.

In 1947, I encountered a superb educator, Josei Toda (1900–58). Toda, together with his mentor, Makiguchi, had been imprisoned for opposing Japan's wars of invasion. Makiguchi died in jail; Toda survived the two-year ordeal of imprisonment. When, aged nineteen, I learned of this, I instinctively knew that here was someone whose actions merited my trust. I determined to follow Toda as my mentor in life. It was Toda's constant and impassioned plea that it was only by fostering new generations of people imbued with a profound respect for the sanctity of life that humanity could be liberated from horrific cycles of war. He therefore gave the highest possible priority to the work of education.

Education is a uniquely human privilege. It is the source of inspiration that enables us to become fully and truly human, to fulfill a constructive mission in life with composure and confidence. When the development of knowledge is isolated from human concerns, it ultimately leads to the creation of weapons of mass destruction. But, at the same time, it is knowledge that has made society comfortable and convenient, bringing industry and wealth. The fundamental task of education must be to ensure that knowledge serves to further the cause of human happiness and peace: it must be the propelling force for an eternally unfolding humanitarian quest. It is for this reason that I consider education the final and most crucially important undertaking of my life. This is also the reason I deeply concur with the view expressed by President Levine that while education is perhaps the slowest means to social change, it is the only means.

Global society today faces myriad interlocking crises. These include wars, environmental degradation, the North-South development gap, divisions among people based on differences of ethnicity, religion, or language. The list is long and familiar, and the road to solutions may seem all too distant and daunting. In my opinion, the root of all these problems is our collective failure to make the human being, human happiness, the consistent focus and goal in all fields of endeavor. The human being is the point to which we must return and from which we must depart anew. What is required is a human transformation—a human revolution.

There are many areas of commonality in the thinking of Makiguchi and Dewey, and this is one of them. They shared an immovable conviction in the need for new modes of people-centered education. As Dewey put it, "Everything which is distinctly human is learned."[1] Dewey and Makiguchi were contemporaries. On opposite ends of the earth, amid the problems and dislocations of their newly industrializing societies, both wrestled with the task of laying a path toward a hope-filled future. Greatly influenced by the views of Dewey,

Makiguchi asserted that the purpose of education must be the lifelong happiness of learners. He further believed that true happiness is to be found in a life of value creation. Put simply, value creation is the capacity to find meaning, to enhance one's own existence and contribute to the well-being of others, under any circumstance. Makiguchi developed his unique educational philosophy while exploring the deep insights Buddhism offers into the inner workings of life.

Both Dewey and Makiguchi looked beyond the limits of the nation-state to new horizons of human community. Both, it could be said, had a vision of global citizenship, of people capable of value creation on a global scale.

Elements of Global Citizenship

What then, are the conditions for global citizenship?

Over the past several decades, I have been privileged to meet and converse with many people from all walks of life, and I have given the matter some thought. Certainly, global citizenship is not determined merely by the number of languages one speaks, or the number of countries to which one has traveled. I have many friends who could be considered quite ordinary citizens but who possess an inner nobility; who have never traveled beyond their native place yet who are genuinely concerned for the peace and prosperity of the world.

I think I can state with confidence that the following are essential elements of global citizenship:

▶ The wisdom to perceive the interconnectedness of all life.
▶ The courage not to fear or deny difference but to respect and strive to understand people of different cultures and to grow from encounters with them.

▶ The compassion to maintain an imaginative empathy that reaches beyond one's immediate surroundings and extends to those suffering in distant places.

The all-encompassing interrelatedness that forms the core of the Buddhist worldview can provide a basis, I feel, for the concrete realization of these qualities of wisdom, courage, and compassion. The following parable from the Buddhist canon provides a beautiful visual metaphor for the interdependence and interpenetration of all phenomena.

Suspended above the palace of Indra, the Buddhist god who symbolizes the natural forces that protect and nurture life, is an enormous net. A brilliant jewel is attached to each of the knots of the net. Each jewel contains and reflects the image of all the other jewels in the net, which sparkles in the magnificence of its totality.

When we learn to recognize what Henry David Thoreau (1817–62) referred to as "the infinite extent of our relations,"[2] we can trace the strands of mutually supportive life and discover there the glittering jewels of our global neighbors. Buddhism seeks to cultivate wisdom grounded in this kind of empathetic resonance with all forms of life. In the Buddhist view, wisdom and compassion are intimately linked and mutually reinforcing. Compassion in Buddhism does not involve the forcible suppression of our natural emotions, our likes and dislikes. Rather, it is the realization that even those we dislike have qualities that can contribute to our lives and can afford us the opportunity to grow in our own humanity. Further, it is the compassionate desire to find ways of contributing to the well-being of others that gives rise to limitless wisdom.

Buddhism teaches that both good and evil are potentialities that exist in all people. Compassion consists in the sustained and courageous effort to seek out the good in any person, whoever they may be, however they may behave. It means striving, through sustained engagement, to cultivate the positive qualities in oneself and in others. Engagement, however, requires courage. There are all too many cases in which compassion, owing to a lack of courage, remains mere sentiment.

Buddhism calls a person who embodies these qualities of wisdom, courage, and compassion, who strives without cease for the happiness of others, a bodhisattva. In this sense, it could be said that the bodhisattva provides an ancient precedent and modern exemplar of the global citizen.

The Buddhist canon also includes the story of a contemporary of Shakyamuni, a woman by the name of Shrimala, who dedicated herself to education, teaching others that the practice of the bodhisattva consists in encouraging, with maternal care, the ultimate potential for good within all people. Her vow is recorded thus: if I see lonely people, people who have been jailed unjustly and have lost their freedom, people who are suffering from illness, disaster, or poverty, I will not abandon them. I will bring them spiritual and material comfort.[3]

In concrete terms, her practice consisted of the following:

▸ Encouraging others by addressing them with kindness and concern, through dialogue (Skt *priyavacana*).
▸ Giving alms, or providing people with the things they require (Skt *dana*).
▸ Taking action on behalf of others (Skt *artha-carya*).
▸ Joining with others, and working together with them (Skt *samanartha*).

Through these efforts, Shrimala sought to realize her goal of bringing forth the positive aspects of those she encountered. The practice of the bodhisattva is supported by a profound faith in the inherent goodness of people. Knowledge must be directed to the task of unleashing this creative, positive potential. This purposefulness can be likened to the skill that enables one to make use of the precision instruments of an airplane to reach a destination safely and without incident. For this reason, the insight to perceive the evil that causes destruction and divisiveness, and that is equally part of human nature, is also necessary. The bodhisattva's practice is an unshrinking confrontation with what Buddhism calls the fundamental darkness of life.

"Goodness" can be defined as that which moves us in the direction of creative coexistence, empathy, and solidarity with others. The nature of evil, on the other hand, is to divide: people from people, humanity from the rest of nature. The pathology of divisiveness drives people to an unreasoning attachment to difference and blinds them to human commonalities. This is not limited to individuals but constitutes the deep psychology of collective egoism, which takes its most destructive form in virulent strains of ethnocentrism and nationalism. The struggle to rise above such egoism and live in larger and more contributive realms of selfhood constitutes the core of the bodhisattva's practice. Education is, or should be, based on the same altruistic spirit as the bodhisattva.

The proud mission of those who have been able to receive education must be to serve, in seen and unseen ways, the lives of those who have not had this opportunity. Although at times education may become a matter of titles and degrees and the status and authority these confer, I am convinced that it should be a vehicle to develop in one's character the noble spirit to embrace and augment the lives of others. In this way, education should provide the momentum to triumph over one's own weaknesses, to thrive in the midst of society's sometimes stringent realities, and to generate new victories for the human future.

The work of fostering global citizens, laying the conceptual and ethical foundations of global citizenship, concerns us all. It is a vital project in which we all are participants and for which we all share responsibility. To be meaningful, education for global citizenship should be undertaken as an integral part of daily life in our local communities.

Like Dewey, Makiguchi focused on the local community as the place where global citizens are fostered. In his 1903 work *Jinsei chirigaku* (The Geography of Human Life), which is considered a pioneering work in social ecology, Makiguchi stressed the importance of the community as the site of learning. Elsewhere, he wrote:

> The community, in short, is the world in miniature. If we encourage children to observe directly the complex relations between people and the land, between nature and society, they will grasp the realities of their homes, their school, the town, village, or city and will be able to understand the wider world.[4]

This is consonant with Dewey's observation that those who have not had the kinds of experience that deepen understanding of neighborhood and neighbors will be unable to maintain regard for people of distant lands.[5]

Our daily lives are filled with opportunities to develop ourselves together with those around us. Each of our interactions with others—dialogue, exchange, and participation—is an invaluable chance to create value. We learn from people, and it is for this reason that the humanity of the teacher represents the core of the educational experience.

Human Education

Makiguchi argued that human education, education that guides the process of character formation, is a transcendent skill that might best be termed an art. His initial experience was as a teacher in Hokkaido, at the time a frontier region of Japan, where he taught classes comprising students from multiple grades. The children were poor, the manners they brought from their impoverished homes rough. Makiguchi, however, was insistent:

> They are all equally students. From the viewpoint of education, what difference could there be between them and other students? Even though they may be covered with dust or dirt, the brilliant light of life shines from their soiled clothes. Why does no one try to see this? The teacher is all that stands between them and the cruel discrimination of society.[6]

The teacher is the most important element of the educational environment. This creed of Makiguchi's is the unchanging spirit of value-creating education. Elsewhere, he wrote:

> Teachers should descend from the throne where they are ensconced like an object of veneration; rather, they should serve those who seek to ascend the throne of learning. They should not be masters who see themselves as the ideal but companions who guide the way toward it.[7]

It is my abiding conviction that it is the teacher dedicated to serving students, and not the inanimate facility, that makes a school. I recently heard an educator assert that students' lives are not changed by lectures but by people. For this reason, interactions between students and teachers are of the greatest importance.

In my own case, most of my education was under the tutelage of my mentor in life, Josei Toda. For some ten years, every day before work, he would teach me a curriculum of history, literature, philosophy, economics, science, and organization theory. On Sundays, our one-on-one sessions started in the morning and continued all day. He was constantly questioning me—interrogating might be a better word—about my reading. Most of all, however, I learned from his example. The burning commitment to peace that remained unshaken throughout his imprisonment was something he carried with him his entire life. It was from this, and from the profound compassion that characterized each of his interactions, that I most learned. Ninety-eight percent of what I am today I learned from him.

The integrated Soka education system, which promotes value creation, was founded out of a desire that future generations should have the opportunity to experience this same kind of human education. It is my greatest hope that the graduates of the Soka schools will become global citizens who can author a new history for humankind.

The actions of such citizens will not be effective unless coordinated, and in this regard we cannot ignore the important potential of the United Nations system.

We have reached the stage where the UN can serve as a center, not only for "harmonizing the actions of nations,"[8] but also for the creation of value through education of global citizens who can create a world of peace. While debate at the world organization has been dominated by states and their national interests, the energy of "We the peoples . . ." has increasingly been making itself felt, particularly through the activities of nongovernmental organizations (NGOs).

In recent years, global discourse on such critical issues as the environment, human rights, indigenous peoples, women, and population has been held under UN auspices. With the participation of both governmental and nongovernmental representatives, conferences on world issues have furthered the process of shaping the kind of global ethic that must undergird global citizenship. In coordination with ongoing efforts of the UN in this direction, I would hope to see these issues incorporated as integral elements of education at all levels. For example:

▸ Peace education, in which young people learn the cruelty and folly of war—to root the practice of nonviolence in human society.

▸ Environmental education—to study current ecological realities and means of protecting the environment.

▸ Developmental education—to focus attention on issues of poverty and global justice.

▸ Human rights education—to awaken an awareness of human equality and dignity.

It has long been my belief that education must never be subservient to political interests. To this end, I feel that it should be accorded a status within public affairs equivalent even to that of the legislative, executive, or judicial branches of government. This proposal grows out of the experiences of my predecessors, Presidents Makiguchi and Toda, who fought consistently against political control of education. In the coming years, I hope that a world summit will be held, not of politicians, but of educators. This is because nothing is of greater importance to the human future than the transnational solidarity of educators. Toward that end, we are determined to continue our efforts to promote educational exchange among young people, following the example of Teachers College, which I understand at present has a student body drawn from some eighty countries.

As Makiguchi stated, "Educational efforts built on a clear understanding and with a defined sense of purpose have the power to overcome the contradictions and doubts that plague humankind and to bring about an eternal victory for humanity."[9]

I would like to pledge my fullest efforts to working, together with my distinguished friends and colleagues gathered here today, toward fostering the kind of global citizens who alone can produce this "eternal victory for humanity."

Realizing a Sustainable Future
Through the Power of Education

On the occasion of the 2002 World Summit on
Sustainable Development.

The Need for Change

MORE THAN TEN years have passed since the holding
of the Earth Summit in Brazil, an event that sparked
sharply increased awareness of the need to protect the
global environment. Since then, the term *sustainable devel-*
opment has become an integral part of our vocabulary, and
on certain fronts, progress has been made. Overall, however,
the agreements reached in Rio have not been kept and the
progress that has been made is not keeping pace with the
degradation of Earth's life systems. It is clear that we cannot
permit this situation to continue further into the twenty-first
century.

Resolving this crisis will require the commitment of more
knowledge, technology, and funds. But what is even more fundamentally lacking in my view are such intangible elements
as a sense of solidarity and common purpose with our fellow
inhabitants of Earth and a real sense of responsibility toward
future generations.

In June of 2002, I had the opportunity to meet with Mr.
Tommy E. Remengesau Jr. (1956–), president of the Republic

of Palau, an island nation often described as a jewel set in the Pacific Ocean. At that time we discussed the environmental crisis and Remengesau shared his deep concerns confirming that global warming is an extremely urgent issue for the people of his nation. He explained that rising tide waters now inundate the islands of Palau, threatening their natural beauty, and that the country is also suffering from drought as a result of the El Niño weather pattern. Rising ocean temperatures are killing off coral reefs, the president added. He also mentioned that Palau is actively engaged in researching and introducing alternative energy sources that reduce greenhouse gases. The times demand this kind of active response—this refusal to be a passive observer or victim of circumstances—not only at the governmental level but also at the grassroots level of civil society.

In the film *A Quiet Revolution,* which was produced by the Earth Council specifically for the 2002 World Summit on Sustainable Development (WSSD), inspiring examples of such action are presented. These include people's responses to the problem of water resources in Nimi Village in India and to the threat of persistent organic pollutants in Zemplínska šírava lake in Slovakia, as well as the example of women who have stood up to protect the forests of Kenya. Our organization, the Soka Gakkai International (SGI), supporting the objectives of this film, cooperated in its production. This is because we believe that the theme running through the film—that a single person can change the world—is the message of courage and hope most needed in these difficult times.

One of the goals of the WSSD was to adopt a plan of implementation that will serve as the basis for making the twenty-first century an era of creative coexistence between humans and nature. UN secretary-general Kofi Annan (1938–2018) had emphasized that the summit would serve as a litmus test for countries' resolve to act.

As part of our efforts to support the WSSD, I offered, in a proposal written earlier in 2002, three suggestions for possible reform of the international system relating to protection of the environment. The first was the appointment of a UN high commissioner for the environment to exercise clear leadership and initiative on global environmental problems. The second was the phased consolidation of the secretariats overseeing the implementation of various environmental treaties, linked to the establishment of a global green fund. The third was the adoption of a convention for the promotion of renewable energy resources.

At the same time, I stressed the need to raise consciousness and change our basic ways of thinking about the environment. In addition to "top-down" reforms, such as the legal and institutional measures outlined above, any lasting solution will require commensurate "bottom-up" reforms that build and strengthen solidarity at the people's level. These are the two interlinked prerequisites of change on a global scale. In this proposal, I would like to focus on the question of how to forge global popular solidarity toward resolution of the global environmental crisis.

International Decade of Education for Sustainable Development

If people are to take environmental issues as their personal concern and to harmonize their efforts for our common future, education is vital. Only education can provide the driving force for such a renewal of awareness. For this reason, the SGI put forward the idea of an international decade of education for sustainable development to follow the UN Decade for Human Rights Education from the year 2005. This proposal was included in the plan of implementation adopted in Johannesburg and, in December 2002, it was approved at the UN General Assembly, with UNESCO named as the coordinating agency. The objectives of the decade would be to promote education as the basis for a sustainable human society and to strengthen international cooperation toward the dissemination of environmental information.

The importance of education for sustainable development was clearly stated in the Agenda 21 plan of action adopted at the 1992 Rio Earth Summit. At the heart of this concept—as stressed in the 1997 Thessaloniki Declaration of the International Conference on Environment and Society—is sustainability. In the words of the declaration: "The concept of sustainability encompasses not only environment but also poverty, population, health, food security, democracy, human rights, and peace." Because environmental issues are so deeply interlinked with these other global issues, their resolution requires a fundamental rethinking of our way of life—as individuals, as societies, and in terms of human civilization itself.

In this sense, I believe the decade of education for sustainable development should be promoted with the following three goals in mind:

- ▸ to **learn** and deepen awareness of environmental issues and realities
- ▸ to **reflect** on our modes of living, renewing these toward sustainability
- ▸ to **empower** people to take concrete action to resolve the challenges we face

To Learn

It is essential to deepen understanding and awareness. Everything starts from grasping basic facts: the amount of the world's forests that have been lost, for example; the degree of pollution of the air, water, and soil; and the overall impact on the global ecosystem.

We also need to understand the causes and social structures driving environmental destruction. And beyond that, we need to learn to empathetically understand the realities of those who suffer, embracing their pain as our own and conscious of our interconnectedness. Such an effort will give birth to renewed awareness and determination to act.

It is vital to incorporate such efforts particularly into the early years of the school curriculum, the stage of growth when children are most rich in their sensitivity, imagination, and creativity, when their desire to learn and absorb is at its height. A number of countries already promote environmental education as an integral part of their school curriculum. To cultivate in children's hearts the desire to treasure nature and protect the earth is a vital step toward protecting their future.

At the Kansai Soka Junior High School in Japan, students have been participating in experiential learning, filming Earth from the space shuttle and international space station as part of NASA's EarthKAM program. As founder of the school, I have been moved and impressed by the educational impact of the children visually confirming evidence of the global environmental crisis through this process.

For some years, I have called for a world summit of educators that would bring together not only those responsible for educational policy in each country but also those engaged on the front lines of education. The start of the Decade of

Education for Sustainable Development (2005) would, I feel, be an appropriate time to hold an international conference where educators from throughout the world could exchange ideas, experiences, and best practices in this area.

At the same time, it is also important that grassroots movements develop opportunities that encourage a deeper understanding of the global environmental crisis. It was to this end that the SGI organized the exhibition *Toward a Century of Hope: Environment and Development* as an official side event of the Rio Earth Summit. In the United States, SGI-USA has created a traveling exhibition titled *Ecology and Human Life*, and the Soka Gakkai in Japan has developed the *EcoAid* exhibition. These efforts, held in cooperation with other NGOs, seek to contribute to public education and enhance awareness at the grass roots.

To Reflect

Together with the provision of accurate information, it is crucial that the ethical values we share are clarified. This is particularly important in the case of environmental issues, which can be so vast and complex that information and knowledge alone can leave people wondering what this all means to them and without a clear sense of what concrete steps they can take. To counter such feelings of powerlessness and disconnection, education should encourage understanding of the ways that environmental problems intimately connect to our daily lives. Education must also inspire the faith that each of us has both the power and the responsibility to effect positive change on a global scale.

The Thessaloniki Declaration states: "Sustainability is, in the final analysis, a moral and ethical imperative in which cultural diversity and traditional knowledge need to be respected." We can learn from the rich spiritual heritage and diverse cultural traditions humanity has fostered over history. From these we can gain precious lessons and philosophical insights into how best to live as human beings.

The Earth Charter, whose drafting was initiated by the secretary-general of the Rio Earth Summit, Maurice Strong (1929–2015), and Green Cross International president Mikhail Gorbachev (1931–), compiles and melds together these many different sources of wisdom. Its four pillars are: (1) respect for all life, (2) ecological integrity, (3) social and economic justice, and (4) democracy, nonviolence, and peace. The Earth Charter offers a comprehensive overview of the values and principles needed for a sustainable future, and as such it is an invaluable educational resource.

In addition to its content, the manner in which this "people's charter" was drafted is significant. In the drafting process, efforts were made to incorporate the essential wisdom of cultures and traditions from all regions of Earth. The language of the drafts was patiently deliberated by experts as well as by many people at the grass roots. To date, the SGI has held workshops and symposiums around the world in an effort to promote and introduce the Earth Charter principles at the grassroots level. I would hope that many efforts would be made to learn from the Earth Charter in programs that link its principles to the specific issues of different communities and their schools.

One of the themes of the Kenyan Green Belt Movement is that the desert does not come from the Sahara—it begins in our backyards. Based on a sense of responsibility toward the future, mothers and children involved in the movement have planted and cared for some twenty million trees. I understand that children who have planted trees often enjoy friendly competition, pouring their love and concern onto the saplings, vying to see whose will grow fastest. Efforts such as this are very significant because it is through such experiences that people—and young people in particular—come to grasp the concrete realities of their community and to sharpen their awareness of the global environment.

The founder of the Soka Gakkai, the Japanese educator Tsunesaburo Makiguchi (1871–1944), described the local community as the world in miniature. He stressed the importance of opening children's eyes to the world through learning rooted in the local community—the place where history, nature, and society intersect.

I believe that this kind of cyclical movement—viewing the world from the perspective of the local community, looking at the community through the lens of the world—is vital if we are to develop an ethical understanding and appreciation of nature that is truly rooted in the felt realities of daily life.

To Empower

Third, people must be empowered with courage and hope if they are to take those first concrete steps. Even if we establish agreed-upon ethics and paradigms of behavior, unless an increasing number of people embody and practice these in their lives, the severe realities we face will not change. In other words, if ethics bear little connection to our individual lives or will but are seen as merely a set of guidelines to be passively followed, an obligation imposed from without, they will not enable us to respond robustly to changing circumstances. They will be abandoned in the first crisis.

It is for this reason that environmental ethics must be felt as a deeply personal vow and pledge, the fulfillment of which provides us with an inexhaustible sense of purpose and joy.

I recently engaged in a dialogue, through meetings and correspondence, with the environmental economist and futurist Hazel Henderson (1933–). She has spoken of her own inspiration to act, drawn from her efforts to protect her daughter from the hazards of air pollution. "Most of us who started Citizens for Clean Air were mothers," she says. "Since we knew what a big task it is to bring up children, we were anxious for our children to have the best futures possible. Thinking back, I realize that's what gave us the strength to endure numerous persecutions and keep pushing ahead."[1]

To be effective, ethics must be charged with this kind of natural and spontaneous sentiment—the irresistible impulse to act that moves us when we see the people and the world we love exposed to danger. Living ethics such as these are truly integrated into the very fiber of our humanity.

What, then, are the values that can serve to truly unite humanity, to link ordinary citizens in genuine solidarity? At the very heart of the values we seek must be a profound reverence for life itself. Such a sense of respect and reverence can awaken people to a sense of connection with all the forms of life with whom we presently share this earth, as well as a sense of oneness with future generations.

This appreciation of the unity and connectedness of life has been a part of many cultural traditions since ancient times; it has been passed on and continues today in many indigenous cultures. It is vital that humanity as a whole humbly attend to this living wisdom. For example, the Desana people of the Amazon say that human beings cannot live in isolation and they can only thrive in harmonious coexistence with their environment. The Iroquois people of North America exhort us to make all decisions keeping in view "not only the present but also the coming generations, even those whose faces are yet beneath the surface of the ground—the unborn of the future." In this worldview, all animals and plants are seen as siblings.

A Contributive Way of Life

This reverence for life is also stressed in many religious traditions. In the Buddhist tradition that inspires the activities of the SGI, we find these words:

> The seen and the unseen
> Those living near and far away
> Those born and those to-be-born—
> May all beings be at ease.[2]

These words are rooted in the view that all life is interconnected and mutually supporting—a relationship described as "dependent origination" in Buddhism. What is key here is the understanding that the desire for happiness lies at the very heart of our interconnection. It is for this reason the teachings of Buddhism stress our role as the protagonists of positive change. While recognizing the influence that our surroundings have on us, the focus is more on our active and conscious engagement with our environment and with other forms of life. The powerful will that drives this dynamic process of change is the concern and compassion we muster for others.

Through dialogue and engagement, we draw forth and inspire in ourselves and in the lives of others a profound sense of purpose and joy. We begin a process of fundamental change that awakens a vastly expanded sense of identity—our "greater self." The ultimate objective of the SGI's activities is to bring about—starting with a reformation or "human revolution" in our individual lives—a universal flowering of the philosophy of reverence for life.

In his 1930 book, *Soka kyoikugaku taikei* (The System of Value-Creating Pedagogy), Tsunesaburo Makiguchi called for a fundamental transformation in the way people live their lives. He decried a passive, dependent way of life and declared that even an active, independent way of life is insufficient. Instead he called for a consciously interactive, interdependent mode of existence, a life of committed contribution.

A passive and dependent way of life lacks a clearly defined sense of self; we live at the mercy of changing circumstance. An independent mode of living may manifest a clear sense of individual self but lack awareness of the realities and needs of others. In contrast, a contributive way of life is based on an awareness of the interdependent nature of our lives—of the relationships that link us to others and our environment. It is a way of life in which we actively strive to realize happiness both for ourselves and for others.

Such a way of life is centered on what we now call empowerment, in particular through the kind of dialogue that unleashes our vast inner potential, inspiring people to work together for the peace and happiness of the entire global community.

Here I am reminded of the words of Aurelio Peccei (1908–84), cofounder of the Club of Rome, whose report "The Limits to Growth" awakened the world to the environmental crisis. In a dialogue we shared, Dr. Peccei stated: "The gamut of still dormant capacities available in each individual is so great that we can make of them the greatest human resource. It is by grooming and developing these capacities in a way consistent with our new condition in this changed world—and only in this way—that we can again put a modicum of order and harmony in our affairs, including our relations with Nature, and thus move safely ahead."[3]

Nothing is more crucially important today than the kind of human education that enables people to sense the reality of interconnectedness, to appreciate the infinite potential in each person's life, and to cultivate that dormant human potential to the fullest.

No matter how complex global challenges may seem, we must remember that it is we ourselves who have given rise to them. It is therefore impossible that they are beyond our power as human beings to resolve. Refocusing on humanity, reforming and opening up the inner capacities of our lives—this kind of individual human revolution can enable effective reform and empowerment on a global scale.

To express my heartfelt wishes for the successful implementation of all the plans agreed at the WSSD, I would like to share these words of my dear late friend, poet laureate of Denmark, Dame Esther Gress (1921–2002):

> If you want to change the world
> you must change man.
> If you want to change man
> you must make him want to.[4]

And I would like to offer these words of the renowned Nigerian writer Ben Okri (1959–), from his poem dedicated to the new century:

> You can't remake the world
> without remaking yourself.

Each new era begins within.
It is an inward event,
with unsuspected possibilities
for inner liberation.[5]

Reviving Education:
The Brilliance of the Inner Spirit

January 9, 2001.

THE TWENTY-FIRST CENTURY is upon us at last. In the autumn of 2000, I presented a paper on education out of a desire to see this new century become "a century of education." My aim was twofold: to sound the alarm in Japan over the continuing treatment of education as simply a means to an end, and to call for a shift from viewing education as serving the narrowly defined needs of society to a new paradigm that sees society serving the lifelong process of education. I believe it is vital that education be reoriented to its prime objective, namely, the lifelong happiness of learners. In this paper, I wish to delve further into the problems of education against which schools and society must be vigilant if we are to find a solution to the bullying and other acts of violence that most immediately and directly affect children.

Incidents of bullying and other forms of physical and psychological violence have been on the rise for some time in Japan, despite the ideal of schools being havens of the joys of learning and living. The Ministry of Education's 1999 survey of public schools from elementary through high school levels reported a record thirty-six thousand incidents of violent behavior, the highest to date. And although the numbers appear to be on a slightly downward trend, well over thirty thousand cases of physical and psychological bullying were reported. This is a deplorable situation. Some observers claim this represents merely the tip of the iceberg, since the numbers do not hint at how many incidents go unreported, let alone how many occur in private schools. Scrutiny of the numbers aside, the point here is that aberrant conditions have become the norm. Children are the microcosm of the times, and, as such, they mirror the future of society. As long as these mirrors remain dark and clouded, we will not see in them a hope-filled future.

While some remedial measures have been instituted by the Ministry of Education and independent commissions, I feel that along with structural deterrents to bullying there is an urgent need to establish, not only in schools but throughout society, an ethos of zero tolerance toward violence.

An Earnest Wish to End Violence

Tsunesaburo Makiguchi (1871–1944), the Japanese educator and founding president of the Soka Gakkai, lamented the plight of the children of his day whose education and very lives bore the imprint of the march toward imperial expansion. This was a man who cherished a deep desire to resolve the underlying problems that were causing intense suffering to an entire generation of ten million children and students exposed to the pressures of a society in turmoil. He was determined that the burden of these problems not be passed on to the next generation. From this vow was born his key work on education, *Soka kyoikugaku taikei* (The System of Value-Creating Pedagogy), published more than seventy years ago in 1930. Central to his formulation of *soka*, or value-creating, pedagogy is the tenet that all children should be afforded the opportunity to limitlessly develop their potential and lead fulfilling lives undeterred by the destructive influences in society. This tenet continues to be the driving force of Soka schools today.

We must end the tragedy of school violence whereby the rich seeds of future promise and potential are destroyed by the children themselves. Every time I visit the Soka schools in Tokyo and Kansai, I speak frankly with the students, stating that bullying and violence are in all cases wrong and encouraging the students that we should all work together to eliminate these evils from society. Of course, there is nothing particularly novel about this appeal. For the vast majority of the adult population, there is a commonsense assumption that the rejection of violence is a cornerstone of civilized society. Unfortunately, of late it seems we can no longer assume this to be the norm of social behavior. The problem of school violence and other acts of juvenile crime and misconduct is not defined simply by the frequency of its occurrence, whether documented incidents have increased or decreased in recent years. Rather, we must examine closely the specific nature of the problem. Unless we squarely face this reality, any appeal to end bullying will fall short of reaching children's hearts and, instead, will have the hollow ring of a superficial slogan.

Above all, we need courage if we are to end violence in schools—the kind of courage that will allow us neither to yield when confronted by evil nor to remain idle witnesses in the face of evil. When we muster up this kind of courage, bullying as well as all other forms of violence will inevitably be rejected. The question is whether we can indeed summon this courage. On the subject of bullying, last year the *Seikyo Shimbun,* the Soka Gakkai's daily newspaper, published a series of discussions between me and several young people regularly in contact with junior high school students. From these talks I became acutely aware of how difficult it is—for parents and teachers as well as for students—to be truly courageous individuals.

The French philosopher and religious writer Simone Weil (1909–43) astutely observed that for writers of her day "words which contain a reference to good and evil" had become "degraded, especially those which refer to the good."[1] We see this increasingly in our own time, when words related to good—not only *courage* but also *effort, patience, love,* and *hope*—are met with cynicism and indifference. Ours is a social climate in which people are perhaps fearful of being judged by others and hesitate even to utter such words. Unless we boldly confront cynicism and indifference, we will be unable to find fundamental and effective responses.

This undercurrent of social and spiritual malaise has spread rapidly in recent years. The question "Why is it wrong to kill people?" was asked recently on a popular Japanese television program. It then became the title of a feature series in a magazine and was later published as a book.[2] These phenomena give us an indication of where the problem lies: when even the time-honored tenets and virtues articulated in all the major world religions, such as prohibitions against the taking of human life, are called into question, one can easily imagine the prevailing attitude toward coercive and violent behavior such as bullying. I believe we must wake up to the fact that cynicism and indifference erode society at its roots and are potentially more dangerous than any individual act of evil.

Two men with whom I have conducted dialogues that have subsequently been published, the renowned Russian children's author Albert A. Likhanov (1935–) and Norman

Cousins (1915–90), known as the conscience of America, both shared this view. They adamantly warned against the dangers of indifference and cynicism in the face of evil—even more than evil itself—because these attitudes reveal a decisive lack of passionate engagement with life, an isolation and withdrawal from reality. Citing the paradoxical words of Bruno Jasieński (1901–38), Mr. Likhanov warns of the profound harm apathy inflicts on a young person's soul:

> Do not fear your enemies. The worst they can do is kill you. Do not fear friends. At worst, they may betray you. Fear those who do not care; they neither kill nor betray, but betrayal and murder exist because of their silent consent.[3]

In other words, averting our eyes from acts of murder or betrayal is what allows such evil to proliferate without end. Similarly, Professor Cousins makes reference to the following statement by Robert Louis Stevenson (1850–94): "I hate cynicism a great deal more than I do the devil, unless perhaps the two are the same thing."[4] He voices his own deep concern that the defeatism and self-doubt characteristic of a pessimistic attitude will undermine and destroy such values as idealism, hope, and trust. A state of life controlled by apathy and cynicism grows immune to emotions of love or hatred, suffering or joy, and retreats into a barren, makeshift world of alienation. Indifference toward evil implies an indifference toward good. It makes for a bleak state of life and a semantic space estranged from the vital drama of the struggle between good and evil.

Children's keen senses quickly detect the apathy and cynicism rampant in an adult world bereft of values. It is perhaps for this reason that adults become uneasy when they see in children's hearts an eerie and familiar darkness.

Evil, like good, is an undeniable reality. Without evil there is no good, and without good there is no evil: they coexist and are defined by their complementarity. Depending on one's response or reaction, evil can be transformed to good or good to evil. In this sense, they are both relative and transmutable. We must therefore recognize that both good and evil are defined in relation to their opposite or "other," and that the "self" is defined by this dynamic.

In Buddhism, we find the concepts of "the oneness of good and evil" (*zen'aku-funi*) and "the fundamental neutrality of life with regard to good and evil" (*zen'aku-muki*). As an example, for the historical Buddha Shakyamuni (representing good) to complete his Buddhist practice and thereby attain enlightenment there had to exist an opposing, evil "other," in this case his cousin Devadatta, who sought to undermine and then destroy him. In contrast, the failure to acknowledge and reconcile oneself with the existence of an opposing "other" is the basic flaw in an apathetic, cynical approach to life, in which only the isolated self exists.

A truer, fuller sense of self is found in the totality of the psyche that is inextricably linked to "other." Carl Jung (1875–1961) distinguished between "ego," which knows only the outer content of the psyche, and "self," which knows its inner content as well and unifies the conscious and the unconscious. In the world of apathy and cynicism we find only an isolated sense of self roaming the superficies of the conscious mind—what Jung refers to as ego. The "self" lacking identification with the "other" is insensitive to the pain, anguish, and suffering of the "other." It tends to confine itself to its own world, either sensing threat in the slightest provocation and triggering violent behavior, or nonresponsively turning away in detachment. I would venture to say this mentality provided the nesting ground of the fanatical ideologies, such as fascism and bolshevism, which swept through the twentieth century. We have more recently witnessed the birth of virtual reality, which can also, I believe, further obscure the "other." Viewed in this light, it is clear that none of us can remain a mere spectator or view the problematic behavior of children as someone else's responsibility.

In the course of our discussion, peace scholar Johan Galtung (1930–) mentioned that the prerequisite for an "outer dialogue" is an "inner dialogue."[5] If the concept of "other" is absent from "self," true dialogue cannot take place. Exchanges between two individuals both lacking a sense of "other" might appear to be dialogue but are in fact simply the trading of one-sided statements. Communication inevitably fails. Most distressing in this kind of semantic space—at once voluble and empty—is that words lose their resonance and are eventually stifled and expire. The demise of words naturally means the demise of an essential aspect of our humanity—the capacity for language that earned us the name *Homo loquens* (speaking man). Reality can be revealed only through genuine dialogue, where "self" and "other" transcend the narrow limits of ego and fully interact. This inclusive sense of reality expresses a human spirituality abounding in vitality and empathy.

In a lecture I delivered at Harvard University in 1991, I stated that the times require an ethos of "soft power." I suggested that an inner-motivated spirituality constitutes the essence of soft power and that this derives from inner-directed processes. It becomes manifest when the soul has struggled through phases of suffering, conflict, ambivalence, mature deliberation, and finally, resolution.

It is only in the burning furnace of intense, soul-baring exchanges—the ceaseless and mutually supporting processes of inner and outer dialogue between one's "self" and a profoundly internalized "other"—that our being is tempered and refined. Only then can we begin to grasp and fully affirm the reality of being alive. Only then can we bring forth the brilliance of a universal spirituality that embraces all humankind.

The Inner Realm of the Soul and Religious Sentiment

I believe that the spiritual heritage of humanity can be found in its great works of literature, which may be considered the quintessential representation of the inner self. Here, I would like to draw on *The House of the Dead*, a work said to have marked a turning point in the career of the great Russian author Fyodor Dostoyevsky (1821–81). The young Dostoyevsky was sentenced, for allegedly harboring revolutionary ideas, to four years of hard labor in the bitter cold of Siberia. *The House of the Dead* is unparalleled in documenting the common virtues of humankind revealed to him through this terrible ordeal.

> [T]he common people . . . never reproach a criminal with the crime that he has committed, whatever it may be. They forgive him in consideration of the sentence passed upon him.
> It is well known that the common people throughout Russia call crime a "misfortune," and the criminal

an "unfortunate." This definition is expressive and profound, though unconscious and instinctive.[6]

The "unfortunate" is an unusual choice of words yet rich in significance. Perhaps it shows Dostoyevsky's somewhat romantic view of the Russian people. Be that as it may, I trust the insight of a great writer who goes beyond the superficial to speak of the inner realm of the soul. To call a crime a "misfortune" and a criminal an "unfortunate" reflects a breadth of perception inclusive of "other." No distinction is made between oneself and the criminal; the expression exudes a sense of empathetic connection.

When empathy remains high even in the midst of adversity, a healthy flow of communication prevails. On the other hand, the loss of a sense of connection between people signals the breakdown of communication in a society. Unable to communicate, to recognize the worth of an individual life, people find themselves endlessly debating—and incapable of answering—the straightforward question "Why is it wrong to kill?"

Thoughtless arrogance, the root of all ideological evil, presupposes that oneself is good and the "other" is evil. By contrast, the kind of attitude described by Dostoyevsky enables one to see that a person compelled by circumstances toward evil can also be inspired toward good. From this view emanates the expansive "inner impulse of compassion"[7] that the French thinker Jean-Jacques Rousseau (1712–78) deemed the primordial foundation of society.

This natural compassion resonates closely with what Mahayana Buddhism terms the *bodhisattva way*, the epitome of which may be found in the words of Bodhisattva Vimalakirti— "Because all living beings are sick, therefore I am sick"[8] —

and in the example of Jesus of Nazareth who focused more love and compassion on the one "lost sheep" than all the rest. The running theme in Dostoyevsky's later works is theodicy, a defense of God's justice in creating a world in which both good and evil exist, and central to Rousseau's thoughts on education is a religious sentiment independent of, and unbounded by, church dogma and authority. It would seem that at the heart of universal feelings of empathy and spirituality thrives some form of religious sentiment and that this is inherent in human beings.

In the twentieth century, a century of war and violence, we find also the bright light of spirituality emanating from the nonviolent struggles of Mahatma Gandhi (1869–1948) and Martin Luther King Jr. (1929–68). One might ask how their struggles became mass movements and why many people today embrace nonviolence. Like Gandhi, who asserted that religion "provides a moral basis to all other activities which they otherwise lack,"[9] I believe the answer is in what lay beneath the words and actions of these leaders. They each based themselves on a strong religious conviction, which enabled them to remain unswayed by any adversity.

The American psychologist Abraham H. Maslow (1908–70) offered an important insight into education from the perspective of spirituality. He stated that the primary consideration of education is to "help [the student] to become the best he is capable of becoming, to become actually what he deeply is potentially."[10] His view closely parallels Makiguchi's approach that consistently placed the happiness of learners at the center of education. Maslow insisted that we must never take our eyes off the "far goals" and "ultimate values" of education, lest we lose sight of the "highest potential" attainable by human beings and end up confusing our priorities.[11] Arguably Japan, with its current educational crisis, should find his warning disquieting. After all, it is a crisis brought on by decades of educational policies shaped by the perceived immediate needs of either the military or the economy. In my view, the long-term values Maslow approached from philosophical, religious, humanistic, and ethical angles equate with the cultivation of spirituality and broad religious sentiment.

In November 2000, I had the opportunity to meet with Professor Victor Kazanjian, dean of Religious and Spiritual Life at Wellesley College, Massachusetts, and one of the cofounders of the Education as Transformation Project. With some 350 participating colleges and universities across the United States, the project seeks to redress the current state of education in which ties between individuals and between individuals and society have eroded. It aims for the embrace of wholeness and spirituality in education. Dean Kazanjian has noted the increasing dissociation between intellectual training and spiritual values, along with the growing trend that views education simply as a means or instrumentality. Consequently, he has expressed high hopes for the humanistic approach to education that Soka University of America will embody, the emphasis on nurturing the whole individual. In fact, this aim is the heart and guiding ethic of *soka*, or value-creating education, which has been painstakingly developed since Makiguchi's time.

The turmoil in education and the consequent darkness enveloping the lives of children point to an eroded ability to educate on the part of society as a whole and its constituent elements—not only those institutions with formal responsibility for educational and religious matters but including the family and the community. We cannot continue merely treating the symptoms of this malaise. I am not alone in believing we have reached the point at which we must opt for a comprehensive strategy. Maslow aptly raised the question of whether a "value-free education" is at all desirable. Perhaps it is time to choose a response that resonates with the spirituality and faith in the depths of the human heart.

I would like to be very clear about this point: in no way am I proposing a return to formal, state-sanctioned religious education in Japan. To do so would be to ignore the painful lessons of the enshrinement of State Shinto as the official religion in pre–World War II Japan. This had, of course, an overwhelming impact on schools at the time, turning them into a delivery system for force-feeding the population with militarism and nationalism. Both the postwar Japanese Constitution and the Fundamental Law of Education expressly prohibit religious education in public schools, and for good reason.

Lately, we hear from certain quarters in Japanese society the resurgent strains of ultranationalism. These voices call for the reinstatement of religious education in public schools as a means to restore social discipline. I am adamantly opposed to repeating the tragic manipulation of young minds that took place in prewar Japan. I am absolutely against compulsory religious education that would trample on the freedoms of thought and religion.

The Soka Gakkai's commitment to human rights can be traced to the spiritual struggles waged by its first president, Tsunesaburo Makiguchi, and its second president, Josei Toda (1900–58). Both men gave their all to combat the totalitarianism that robbed citizens of their spiritual freedom and mobilized the Japanese nation into war. As heir to their spiritual legacy, I believe standing up for religious freedom to be an important role of the Soka Gakkai in society. This has also

REVIVING EDUCATION ✳ 41

been my personal commitment. Twenty-seven years ago, in December 1973, addressing the organization's annual headquarters general meeting, I gave voice to this credo:

> Obviously, we must do all we can to ensure our own freedom of religion and faith. But in addition, should it ever become apparent that the authorities are trying to use violence to rob others of their spiritual freedom, even if the philosophies and faiths of those people differ from ours, we must offer them all the protection we can in the name of the dignity of man. Because this is the unaltering Buddhist view of humanity, I insist that we must afford our protection to those whose religions are different from our own and even to those who reject religion altogether.

Freedom of religion, though guaranteed by the Japanese Constitution, cannot be taken for granted. For this reason, I have made it a point to speak out in protest against religious education in public schools. The proposition infringes basic rights and runs counter to the Fundamental Law of Education, Article IX, which reads: "The schools established by the state and local public bodies shall refrain from religious education or activities for a specified religion."[12]

Of course, unlike public schools, private schools can provide religious education when it accords with their educational philosophies, goals, and religious values. This is not a cause for concern as long as the children's personal freedom of religion is not infringed. On this point, the Soka schools form part of a private educational system ranging from kindergarten to the university level, and they focus on value-creating education. Religious doctrine is not taught in Soka schools, nor is it incorporated into any class. With the aim of developing students' abilities to ponder meaning and purpose, the schools' mission is to foster a rich humanity and spirituality that will enable students to create value within and for the benefit of society.

The Cultivation of Spirituality

How to inspire spirituality and religious sentiment is a challenge that has exercised humanity throughout history. I maintain that if we are to revive in education its ability to foster spirituality and broad religious sentiment, every individual, every family, every organization, and every sector of society must pool their energies and resources. Naturally the Soka Gakkai International shares in this challenge as a Buddhist-based movement promoting transformation of the individual and engagement with society. In other words, the role of religion is inseparable from the individual and society: religion must enable individuals to achieve their personal goals as well as contribute positively to society. Were these intertwining paths to diverge, religious sentiment would be reduced to sectarianism; religion would degenerate into something antihuman and antisocial. Any religious movement that considers its role and mission as separate from society is, in my view, making a fundamental error. There is a sharp distinction between the broad religious sentiment I describe here and narrow sectarianism.

Any religious sentiment that does not enable individuals to create value or take constructive action in their personal lives and in society is deceptive and does not deserve to be called religious at all. At the organization's annual headquarters general meeting held in November 1975, I described the mission of the Soka Gakkai as follows: "Various powers in the world—authority, money, brutality—attempt to violate human dignity. The role of the Soka Gakkai in society is to employ the spirit that wells from the very depths of life to do battle with such powers."

During the Kobe earthquake of 1995, the local Soka Gakkai members, spearheaded by the youth, contributed significantly and immediately by providing voluntary assistance to those afflicted. Soka Gakkai community centers served as emergency shelters, and hot meals were provided. Likewise, in September 2000, Soka Gakkai members participated in relief efforts to distribute welcome aid when torrential rains hit the eastern coastal regions of Japan. I believe that such actions, sharing in both the sorrows and joys of other people, are the natural expression of spirituality and religious sentiment.

Whether a religion can move beyond sectarianism and whether the spirituality and religious sentiment it inspires can garner universal understanding will be the test of that faith tradition's ability to contribute to civilization in the twenty-first century. This is the reason I must state once more my grave concerns regarding the dangers of reintroducing sectarian religious education into public schools.

I believe that the means to encourage a flowering in the neglected inner lives of children will always be exposure to literature and the arts. In short, I believe the key is to be found in reading books. The first step in reviving dialogue where human bonds and communication have broken down is to revitalize and infuse the written and spoken word with the light of spirituality. Literary masterpieces are the ideal vehicle for this endeavor, which should not be limited to schools. From my own experience, I can say that immersing oneself in the world's greatest literature at a young age is an invaluable, lifelong asset.

In Japan, the school system affords children various opportunities to read literature. In many cases, however, these works are delivered in the form of Japanese-language textbooks designed mainly to improve reading skills. More reading programs are now being instituted in schools across Japan, but perhaps the aim should be higher: serious consideration should also be given to making world literature a core subject in the school curriculum.

In the Swedish school system, the curriculum is designed to reflect no bias in favor of any specific religion. Student motivation and initiative to read are central to the educational program, in that students are given the freedom to select topics of interest from a broad range of texts. Encouraging the children in this way hones their powers of insight and reasoning, so they are equipped to grapple with the fundamental and ethical issues facing modern civilization. As Japan reexamines educational methods and their implementation, it can benefit greatly from the examples of other countries.

In a sense, reading gives us an insight into the author's life experiences. In *Nagai saka* (The Long Slope), popular novelist Shugoro Yamamoto (1903–67) notes:

> Life is long. Whether one reaches the summit in one bound or steadily scales the mountain step by step, the destination is the same. Rather than accomplishing the journey in one bound, scaling the mountain step by step affords one the opportunity to enjoy the scenery along the way. The trees. The plants. The springs. Moreover, one can have confidence in knowing that each step has been taken carefully and securely. This becomes the source of greater strength.[13]

His imaginative and profound words can be applied easily to the experience of reading. Reading the classics is challenging. Even when they are not lengthy, grasping their essence is not as easy as it is for, say, comic books. A complex passage may require rereading two or three times before it makes some kind of sense. Some passages may defy immediate comprehension, requiring instead the light of time. Certainly, these arduous efforts are much like those of a mountain climber who carefully checks for secure footing and remains alert to his surroundings as he makes his way to the summit. Digests or synopses of great works do them no justice. Only when we have painstakingly struggled to grasp the full meaning of a book does it become part of our flesh and blood.

The value of the reading experience when shared with friends or teachers is greater than that when reading in isolation. It is heightened by the exchange of ideas, especially when one considers reading a lifelong habit. My own teenage years, spent amid the ash and rubble of the postwar period, were enriched immeasurably by a reading circle formed with the youth in my neighborhood. Also, forever etched in my life are precious memories of reading sessions with my mentor, Josei Toda. My mentor never tired of encouraging me to be an active reader—to strive to absorb but not be overwhelmed by books. A master of life, he taught me through his attitude and words this invaluable lesson: the way we relate to books is the way we relate to people, and encountering a good book is the same as encountering a good mentor or a good friend.

I have a second reason for insisting on the importance of reading. An accumulation of experience of reading can act as a buffer to shield one's inner life from the adverse influences of what is popularly termed *virtual reality*. Clearly, the projection of images in virtual reality has some utilitarian value. But it is also true that it distorts as well as simulates real-life experiences in which people share an empathic resonance through direct contact with one another and with nature. On the purely harmful side, the overpowering stimulation and excitement virtual reality produces can lull the imagination and numb sympathetic feelings for real pain and suffering. Once inured to the conditioning of virtual reality, people may turn into mere passive receptors of programmed images. Active faculties, components of an inner-motivated spirituality—the powers, for example, to think critically, to make decisions, to love and empathize, to stand against evil, to believe—tend to atrophy.

The French scientist and philosopher Albert Jacquard (1925–2013) has made the following observation:

> Information science, inasmuch as it provides information, is valuable. However, it supplies only communication canned or frozen. It is incapable of evoking the bursts of creativity that come naturally in the course of a dialogue comprising moments of silence as well as words.[14]

His way of describing dehumanized communication is very apt. Reading, on the other hand, generates a restorative breeze of inspiration in the depths of one's soul—a capacity well beyond that of such "frozen" communication. After all, the experience of reading comes down to a tenacious, intimate dialogue between author and reader. This is the reason I refer to the world of reading as a rich summation of life experiences.

Yet another reason to value reading is that it affords youth and adults alike the opportunity to rise above the routine experiences of everyday life and ponder their past and future prospects. Be it from a book previously read or one pored over for the first time, we feel something genuine, we are moved as every fiber of our being grapples with its content. Without such full engagement, it would be nearly impossible to share our impressions of books with children. The truth resonates with the listener not through empty words but through the richness and depth of one's own character. Above all else, the experience of reading nurtures the spontaneity of children's curiosity. It encourages their self-discipline to take time for reflection and develops their capacity to seek solutions from within.

Tolstoy's Portrait of Spiritual Transformation

World literature is a treasure house of questions, of reflection and wonderment.

Let us draw from a scene in the final chapter of Tolstoy's (1828–1910) *Anna Karenina*, where the protagonist, Levin, asks himself: "What am I? And where am I? And why am I here?"[15] Levin, said to portray Tolstoy himself, is seeking the reason for his existence when he encounters a peasant whose words transform him. Tolstoy deftly and poignantly captures this transformation, the opening of new horizons and the subsequent opening and flowering of Levin's emotions:

> Well, that's how it is—people are different. One man just lives for his own needs, take Mityukha even, just stuffs his belly, but Fokanych—he's an upright old man. He lives for the soul. He remembers God.[16]

To live for one's soul—these simple words, spoken nonchalantly by a peasant, pierce Levin's heart. Walking along the road, he continues his soliloquy as he savors this novel sensation.

He felt something new in his soul and delightedly
probed this new thing, not yet knowing what it was.[17]

As he finally becomes satisfied that he has gleaned the
answer, Levin turns into the woods to lie down on the grass
and thinks to himself:

I haven't discovered anything. I've only found out
what I know. I've understood that power which not
only gave me life in the past but is giving me life now.
I am freed from deception, I have found the master.[18]

Images of transformation from darkness to light appear frequently in Tolstoy's works, typically from questioning to effu-
sive inspiration from the contact of two souls, then through
self-examination to the discovery and formation of a new self.
These processes truly capture the workings of the spirit.

By virtue of his vital spirituality regained, Levin sees through
the deception of war to its harsh and simple reality—human
beings killing one another. The dawning truth seeps into his
interjection: "But it's not just to sacrifice themselves, it's also
to kill Turks."[19] His observation casts doubt on the legitimacy
of the nationalistic fervor that made self-sacrifice in the Ser-
bian War a noble undertaking. The eternal commandment
"Thou shalt not kill" gains new meaning and is imbued with
a sense of immediacy when invoked by one like Levin who has
lived through spiritual agony and torment.

What I regard as the climactic point of the story appears in
the closing scene, where Levin bares his doubts:

As he was going into the nursery, he remembered what
he had hidden from himself. It was that if the main
proof of the Deity is His revelation of what is good,

then why was this revelation limited to the Christian Church alone?[20] . . .

"Well, but the Jews, the Mohammedans, the Confucians, the Buddhists—what are they? . . . Can these hundreds of millions of people be deprived of the highest good, without which life has no meaning?"[21]

I regard Tolstoy's *Anna Karenina* as unparalleled in its portrayal of the spirituality and religious sentiment residing in every human soul.

The extent to which serious reading and appreciation of literature can enrich and create substance in our inner world defies description. Allowing our common spiritual heritage to go to waste would be a source of deep regret. This is true not only of Tolstoy's works. The same can be said of books by Dostoyevsky, Hugo (1802–85), and Goethe (1749–1832), among many others. For decades, even centuries, these classics, rich with substance, have stood the test of time. For anyone who finds world literature daunting, there are modern classics in one's own language and children's books such as those recommended by the Jungian psychologist Hayao Kawai (1928–2007) in Japan. The choices are endless.

There are those who would say we have become distant from the printed word. I share this concern, and it is for just this reason that I wish to extol the value of reading in one's youth. It is truly sad to find young people who have not experienced the thrilling challenge of mastering even one literary classic. It is my abiding hope that preschoolers and schoolchildren be afforded every opportunity to be exposed to reading at home as well as in school. While there is much children gain from reading on their own, the experience is further enriched when parents and teachers read aloud to them.

Children sense the warmth of words in the voices of their

parents and teachers, and their imagination is challenged to capture a story's landscapes and dramatic scenes. The modulations of the reader's voice help children experience and develop a range of emotions, from sadness to joy. As parents and teachers read aloud, they can watch the children's facial expressions and choose to change their tone or pause to hear a child's thoughts. Through these encounters, a relationship of mutual trust steadily begins to take shape.

Just as a farmer sows seeds and prays for a bountiful crop, it is important for adults to read to children in the hope that they will grow up healthy and strong, limitlessly develop their potential and realize every dream. Every facet of a child's development depends on that child's reassurance and confidence that someone believes in him or her, that someone cares.

Education and the Future

On a final note, I believe some programs sponsored by the education department of the Soka Gakkai offer one example of reinforcing society's ability to educate.

By way of introduction, in 1968, members of the education department, determined to contribute to their local community, launched an educational counseling program. In the thirty-two years of its existence, this program has provided volunteer educational counseling services to some 280,000 people. At present, eight hundred members of the education department are active as counselors in twenty-eight communities throughout Japan. All are current or retired teachers who have acquired a background in educational counseling. On a weekly basis, they provide counseling to those who are experiencing difficulties within the educational system, reinforcing their skills through peer review of case studies. The program is open to all members of the community, without regard to religious affiliation, and all advice and counseling are given purely from a secular educational perspective.

A further program was launched in 1999 in an effort to support education in the family and the community. A designated senior educational counselor serves as a liaison with the local community, organizing informal discussions on educational issues. Eventually this system will be expanded to reach communities throughout Japan. Due to the steady efforts of the committed individuals involved in this counseling, there are numerous stories of children who have regained their confidence and made a fresh start. To help a suffering child or parent who is feeling isolated because of various difficulties, I believe it is necessary to supplement the counseling provided by schools and by the government. Educational counseling incorporated into community services would make access to professional help easier and less intimidating. In other words, society must draw on collective efforts to help overcome the current problems in education. According to their records, absenteeism or refusal to attend school now accounts for 70 percent of the cases brought to the educational counseling program. In almost half of these cases, fear of bullying is the reason children feel unable or unwilling to go to school.

In the face of these realities, we cannot remain idle. Our whole society must show a greater concern if we are to counter the problems of bullying and other acts of violence. We are in urgent need of a social ethos that will not accept or condone violence in any form. We must reverse the tide of indifference and cynicism now permeating society.

The Soka Gakkai is deeply committed to raising awareness of these problems and to seeking solutions. Its efforts in this area fulfill one dimension of an overall challenge to create a society that serves the needs of education. More broadly, we are confident that these efforts are helping nurture the roots of a culture of peace.

A strengthened capacity to educate, the weaving of education into every thread of our social fabric, the permeation of a sense of commitment and a responsibility to educate—such concrete developments, and not simply politics or the economy, are what will determine the future. Our children's happiness rests in the balance. Qualified only by an overarching commitment to establish this century as the century of education, it is my earnest desire to work together with like-minded people around the world to continually swell the tide of human education.

Building a Society That Serves the Essential Needs of Education

September 29, 2000.

As we enter the twenty-first century, education is once again the focus of considerable discussion. In Japan, this debate has concentrated on educational reform, and I would like to take this opportunity to respond to some points raised recently and offer some frank opinions on this subject, as well as to make some concrete proposals.

One widespread problem recently has been that of children who for various reasons, particularly bullying, refuse to attend school. It is said this problem could affect almost any child in Japan: The Ministry of Education's annual survey of Japanese schools has revealed that absenteeism in elementary and junior high schools reached the unprecedented number of more than 130,000 students in 1999. This means that, at the elementary school level, one out of every 290 students is unable or unwilling to attend school, and, at the junior-high level, one out of forty, an average of one student in every class.

In Japan, there has been a terrible series of school suicides and other tragedies resulting from bullying, and the crisis is escalating, while the worldwide problem of drug abuse is gradually spreading to Japan as well. In addition, a succession of juvenile crimes including a series of murders by fourteen- and fifteen-year-olds has shocked the Japanese public in recent

years. In just the last year, we have seen the motiveless murder of a sixty-five-year-old housewife and the hijacking of an
expressway bus, both by seventeen-year-olds, and the case of a
boy who brutally clubbed his mother to death with a baseball
bat, crimes which would have been practically unthinkable in
Japan just a few years ago.

Professionals in the fields of juvenile psychology and education analyze these issues, looking for solutions. Realistically
speaking, however, adult society has still failed to deal with
these problems. Shocked at their monstrosity, we feel helpless
in the face of these unfathomable trends.

As one individual who aspires to promote the sound growth
of the young people who are to shoulder our future, in 1984
I penned a proposal for a nationwide general meeting of the
Soka Gakkai's education division titled "Humanity in Education." Based on the principle that educational reform should
be driven by human, not political concerns, I outlined in that
proposal a human ideal imbued with creativity, internationalism, and totality.

I recall that at that time, too, the crisis of education was a
matter of major concern, and parents and teachers and many
other concerned individuals were deeply worried about the
issues of problematic behavior, school violence, and absenteeism. More than fifteen years have passed since then, and
sadly, notwithstanding the efforts of those involved, not only
has there been no improvement, but this situation has now
become the norm, and numerous new problems have subsequently emerged.

The Flight From Learning

One of the most serious problems recently has been the breakdown of discipline in schools as classes become uncontrolla-

ble due to students' disruptive behavior. This problem was initially marked at the junior high school level but has been affecting even the elementary school level in recent years. In the worst cases, children are already undisciplinable by the time they enter elementary school from kindergarten, totally disrupting classes. There have even been surveys that show that a third of the homeroom teachers responsible for these children are so frustrated that they have considered giving up altogether. If nothing is done, we may see the dysfunction of the entire school system.

Another acute problem is a decline in academic achievement. Students' aversion to study, as seen in their dislike of subjects such as mathematics and science, is becoming a serious problem. Various studies demonstrate how the academic level of Japanese children is deteriorating altogether and that this is now affecting high school and further education. There are reports, which would almost be laughable if they were not so shocking, of university students who lack a grasp of even the most basic concepts.

I would refer to this situation as a "flight from learning." I don't think it would be overdramatic to describe this trend as the defeat of education, the failure of our education system to fulfill its essential function—namely, the provision of the spiritual nourishment that enables us to develop our creativity through learning from the wisdom of our predecessors and thereby gain access to the common cultural assets that humankind passes down from generation to generation.

In 2002, Japan will complete the phased reduction of the school week to five days from the traditional six. In tandem with this, the Ministry of Education is introducing a revised curriculum aiming to cultivate children's "zest for living" by providing latitude for their growth. This move must, I think, reflect criticism of the conventional cramming method that

places too much emphasis on rote learning and furious examination competition and is among the principal causes of the
flight from learning. There are, however, many doubts as to
whether this change will lead to a genuine revival of learning
or a comprehensive improvement of academic ability among
students. These concerns are based on the possibility that
if the number of classroom hours is reduced as proposed,
rather than promoting voluntary study as intended, it will
most probably result in children either spending more time
in cramming schools or more hours watching television and
playing video games, and thus not necessarily produce the
expected results.

I share these anxieties. Although the suffering of children,
as symbolized by absenteeism, must be tackled immediately, I
cannot possibly believe that the underlying problems can be
fixed just by tinkering with the system. So, what is behind our
children's pathology of staying away from school, of problematic behavior, and the flight from learning, which is rampant
in contemporary society? I believe the fundamental cause is
the overall decline of the educational functions that should
be inherent not only in schools but in our communities, families, and society as a whole.

If it is education in the widest sense that enables human
beings to truly express their humanity, then there must be
a functional disorder in contemporary Japanese society that
prevents individuals from becoming genuinely mature. This
breakdown is manifested most acutely in the most fragile and
sensitive constituent of our society, that is, the children. At
the risk of oversimplification, we must never forget the time-
honored saying "Children are the mirror of society" when
considering the problems of education. Unless adults possess
a kind of self-reflective attitude to correct in themselves that

which is mirrored back to them by their children, attempts to reform the system, however well intentioned, may ultimately end up as stopgap or temporary measures that merely work around the edges of the system.

I found the following words in an article on moral education by the writer Taichi Yamada (1934–) very moving: "Our children need more than empty sermons about virtue. As adults, we must somehow demonstrate to them in practice how to live a better life."[1] The truth is, however, that the adult world that has suddenly been revealed after the end of Japan's period of rapid economic growth and in the aftermath of the collapse of the "bubble" economy is in an extremely wretched and gloomy state, approaching the new century with practically no vitality. Be it in politics, the bureaucracy, business, or the media, the elite have behaved shamefully, totally bent on vindicating themselves, evading social responsibility, and protecting their own interests.

Japanese society is rife with materialism and scandalous corruption among adults, a situation symbolized by a spate of insurance-related murder cases that demonstrate our loss of values and sense of purpose. This has definitely cast a dark shadow in the hearts of our children. In a society lacking role models who can inspire the next generation, of course education cannot function properly. There are doubtless large numbers of individuals who are unaffected by the sensationalism of the media and continue to work sincerely, adhering to a belief that what is essential is, in the words of Yamada, to "demonstrate in practice how to live a better life." Even these people, however, are finding it difficult to uphold their principles. The fact that people increasingly look back upon the Meiji era (1868–1912) with nostalgia reflects that they feel there is a spiritual deficiency in contemporary Japanese society.

A Paradigm Shift

I believe these problems are also part of the reason behind calls for a review and possible amendment of the Fundamental Law of Education, the mainstay of the postwar education system, as part of a series of educational reforms.

The July 2000 report by the prime minister's private advisory board, the National Council on Educational Reform (NCER), stated that the majority view was that an amendment of the Fundamental Law of Education was required, and that "in the preamble and provisions in Article 1, there is an overemphasis on individual and universal humanity and an omission of respect toward the nation, the community, tradition, culture, the home, and nature." In fact, it is hard to find fault with the principles stated in the preamble or in Article 1, which stipulates the objectives of education as follows:

> Education shall aim at the full development of personality, striving to nurture the citizens, sound in mind and body, who shall love truth and justice, esteem individual value, respect labor and have a deep sense of responsibility, and be imbued with the independent spirit, as builders of the peaceful state and society.[2]

This is a perfectly acceptable statement of the universal principle of "full development of personality" based on respect for individual dignity, and is pertinent to peoples of all times and cultures. In applying this universal principle, however, its relevance must be tested in the social and ethical context. I feel in this sense that those who drafted this law were not specific enough. People failed to delve into what the individual in this context really means. In fact, the individual can become fully realized only through interaction with others, and in order to do this it is necessary to control egoism. This is perhaps so self-evident that the drafters of the law failed to pay enough attention to it. They failed to be adequately aware of the dangers of individualism degenerating into selfish egoism.

Thus, any review or revision of the law proposed by the NCER must be based on a clear understanding of the way in which universal principles find expression within cultural particularities. And I believe that this same concern motivated Tatsuo Morito (1888–1984), the minister of education who was instrumental in drafting the Fundamental Law of Education and who later expressed doubts about its effectiveness.

Although not mentioned in the council's report, there is a reactionary mood in the country calling for a return to the spirit of the following section of the Imperial Rescript on Education to correct these deficiencies:

> Ye, Our subjects, be filial to your parents, affectionate to your brothers and sisters; as husbands and wives be harmonious, as friends true; bear yourselves in modesty and moderation; extend your benevolence to all. . . .[3]

Merely filling the text with references to culture, tradition, and the home will not, I think, produce much effect. Without question, reinstatement of the virtues extolled in the Imperial Rescript on Education would be totally anachronistic when one considers the role the Rescript assumed in Japan's imperial and patriarchal systems before and during the war. The Fundamental Law of Education has been the mainstay of the postwar education system in Japan, and for this reason

I believe that any revision should be undertaken only after careful thought and review; hasty revision is to be avoided.

The modern Japanese educational system has reached a critical juncture. We are witnessing the consequences of education being subordinated to various bureaucratic and political agendas under the control of the Ministry of Education.

Modern Japan's progress, whether it be the prewar policy of building national prosperity and military strength or the postwar stress on becoming an economic superpower, has been motivated by an unconditional national imperative to catch up with and surpass the West. At the same time, ever since the Meiji era, education has been coercively positioned as a means to attain these goals. Both of these approaches are now evidently at a stalemate as Japan is compelled to make an orbital change in direction from industrialization to adaptation to the information-oriented era.

Hence, as I consider education in the twenty-first century, I would like to assert that what is most urgently needed is a paradigm shift from looking at education for society's sake to building a society that serves the essential needs of education.

In formulating the conceptual paradigm of a society that serves the essential needs of education, I was inspired by Professor Robert Thurman (1941–) of Columbia University. Each time I have had the chance to meet with him, I have been impressed by the depth of his vision. In an interview with the Boston Research Center for the Twenty-First Century,[4] he was asked how he viewed the role of education in society. He replied, "I think the question should rather be: What is the role of society in education? Because in my view education is the purpose of human life." This is indeed a penetrating insight. Professor Thurman says that this view is largely due to influences from the teachings of Shakyamuni, whom he considers one of humanity's first teachers. This resonates with

Kant's ethical philosophy, which insists that we respect the autonomy of others and that humans must never be used as a means to an end.

Learning is the very purpose of human life, the primary factor in the development of personality, that which makes human beings truly human. Nevertheless, development of personality has consistently been reduced to a subordinate position and viewed as a means to other ends. This view has prevailed worldwide throughout modern history, particularly in the twentieth century. The educational system has therefore been reduced to a mere mechanism that serves national objectives, be they political, military, economic, or ideological. A certain type of personality, not the full development of personality, has been sought, as if casting individuals from a uniform mold. Treating education as a means rather than an end reinforces a utilitarian view of human life itself.

It is a terrible tragedy that the twentieth century suffered ceaseless wars and violence and became an unprecedented era of mass killing. Needless to say, this demonstrates an increase in killing power, the negative legacy of technological advance. Furthermore, I feel that it is in large part due to an overturning of values in modern civilization, caused by ceasing to regard human beings as the basis of value and instead assigning merely subordinate roles to education, which should be a fundamental and primary human activity.

In this regard, I feel some anxiety about attitudes toward the IT revolution. As was described in the Okinawa Charter on Global Information Society at the Okinawa-Kyushu Summit this year, "Information and Communication Technology (IT) is one of the most potent forces in shaping the twenty-first century."[5] There can be no doubt that the IT revolution will become one of the megatrends in the forthcoming century, and it is of course important not to be left behind.

University professors and officials have frequently noted that the deterioration of academic ability among Japanese students, especially in mathematics and sciences, if left unsolved, may negatively affect Japan's economy and technological ability and consequently delay Japan in the worldwide race toward the IT revolution. It is only right to be apprehensive in this regard.

While globalization naturally entails both positive and negative aspects, the current toward internationalization in the twenty-first century will be unstoppable. No country can remain unaffected. Yet my personal uneasiness is about the possibility of retracing the footsteps of the past, that is, returning to the idea of education for society's sake in tackling the problem of how to improve the academic level of our students. Insofar as the IT revolution by nature has the potential to cause a paradigm shift in contemporary society, its influence contains positive and negative potentials. My observation of the current state of affairs, however, is that only the optimistic and positive aspects have been stressed.

In the United States—which anticipated the IT revolution first, especially in the financial sector, and sometimes appears to have carved out for itself a monopoly position where materialism and "casino capitalism" thrive—the darkness of the IT revolution undoubtedly casts a growing shadow. If all that the new invention of IT brings to human society is a tendency toward materialism, then what use is this revolution?

A Society That Confuses Happiness With Pleasure

In the face of this tendency, we need to return to the core issue of human values. I believe we need to redefine the crucial concept of "development of personality." People have come to take this phrase, which the Fundamental Law of Education describes as the purpose of education, for granted. But this is a universal goal that we must strive to realize and implement. It is a fundamental concept, and it can never be emphasized enough as the key to educational reform.

For this purpose, let us experiment by replacing the phrase *development of personality* with the word *happiness*. The first president of the Soka Gakkai, Tsunesaburo Makiguchi (1871–1944), who was an outstanding educator, never ceased to stress that the purpose of education is ensuring children's happiness.

Makiguchi's pedagogy is gradually gaining international recognition today, but it was originally conceived under Japan's prewar militarist regime, which mobilized every educational institution to foster obedient imperial subjects. It was against this process that Makiguchi protested, asserting that education's true aim should be the lifelong well-being of children and critiquing the Imperial Rescript on Education as providing nothing more than a "minimum set of moral standards." In other words, he was a farsighted individual who, during a period of fanatical militarism, held fast to his belief that society should serve the authentic needs of human education and that education must never be sacrificed to nationalistic goals.

Happiness, however, must not be confused with mere pleasure. Mistaking momentary pleasure for a life of genuine satisfaction and happiness exemplifies the skewing of values that in my opinion has been at the root of the distortions of postwar Japanese society. This mistaken attitude results in liberty yielding to indulgence and self-seeking, peace yielding to cowardice and indolence, human rights to complacency, and democracy to mobocracy. Consequently, development of personality ceases, and we are left with immature and arrogant individuals, unable to grow out of their childish ways and never listening to others, as described by José Ortega y Gasset (1883–1955) in *The Revolt of the Masses.*

The experience of a truly human life—genuine happiness—can be realized only in the bonds and interactions between people. Herein lies the essence of the Buddhist perspective on human life and happiness. Enmity, contradiction, and discord may seem to be unavoidable aspects of relations between humans and our relations with nature and the universe. But it is through the process of persevering in spite of this and transforming these conflicts, restoring and rejuvenating the bonds among us, that we are able to forge and polish our individuality and character. If these bonds are severed, the human spirit can only roam aimlessly in the pitch darkness of solitude. In psychological terms this might be referred to as a "communication disorder," a pathology of modern society due to a weakening of the bonds between people.

Antisocial behavior and the increasing viciousness of juvenile crimes are acute manifestations of this social pathology. There is an ongoing debate in Japan about amending the juvenile law, but changing the law will not of itself lead to a solution of the problem. It is the responsibility of adults to patiently restore the ability to communicate by listening to the voices of isolated children calling out for help from the darkness. There is a famous anecdote about Socrates (c. 470–399 BCE) in which his influence on youth is described as being like an electric ray that stings those who touch it. He explains that he can electrify others because he is electrified himself. Similarly, teachers must be constantly creative if they are to evoke creativity in their students. This is an essential quality in an educator. What is most important is the attitude of the teachers themselves. Human interaction is the key.

Communication between humans and the natural environment is also vital. In this respect also, Makiguchi had piercing foresight. At the opening of his book *Jinsei chirigaku* (The Geography of Human Life), Makiguchi stresses the importance of the influence of the natural environment on the development of personality by citing a work by the renowned educator and reformist Yoshida Shoin (1830–59):

People do not develop in isolation from their environment, and human affairs are just a reflection of the people. Therefore, to understand human affairs, you first must understand the local context in which the people have developed.[6]

Makiguchi went on to state that you can foster qualities of compassion, goodwill, friendship, kindness, sincerity, and honesty, and cultivate nobility of the heart, only within the local community.

The Geography of Human Life was published in 1903, more than half a century before environmental issues such as shortages of natural resources and energy and pollution of the atmosphere and water compelled humanity to reconsider our relationship with nature. Even then, Makiguchi keenly perceived that a breakdown of communication with nature not only causes humans physical damage but also results in the destruction of virtues such as compassion that are essential to development of personality.

If the twentieth century was one in which human beings violently destroyed the global environment like rapacious invaders, then maintaining communication and contact with nature is absolutely indispensable in the education of our children and the young people who are to take responsibility for the twenty-first century. Just as with communication among humans, we must increase our opportunities to interact directly with nature, rather than with the world of virtual reality. What can virtual reality offer to compare with the real-life sensation of communicating with nature—breathing the same air and basking in the same sunlight as the earth, trees, grass, and animals—the dynamic expanse of life?

I recall a moving passage from an essay by Nobukiyo Takahashi (1914–2002), an authority on forest research:

> The beauty of the evening forest, especially under a full moon, throws into sharp contrast the boundary between the sky and the mountain ridges, as if viewing a wood-block print. It is a world of white and black. It is also a world savored only by those who experience it. Captured in photos or video, you may be able to discern these images to a certain extent, but you can never feel them in the same way. Because when you are there, it is not only through your eyes that you are touched: your skin senses the temperature and humidity; you smell the evening forest; fleetingly heard sounds that defy definition flit past your ears. Go out into the night forest, pick up a leaf, examine it front and back. How much beauty you can discover![7]

Creative coexistence is clearly one of the key concepts for the twenty-first century, as I stressed in the peace proposal I penned in 1992.

If we are to build a society that serves the essential needs of education in the twenty-first century, we must not become divided or isolated. Rather, we must deepen human bonds that transcend differences of ethnicity and nationality and also be in free and full communication with nature. We must give the highest priority to cultivating in young people the strength of character and values that will enable them to take the lead in building a world of creative coexistence.

The Independence of Education

Next, I would like to raise a few specific suggestions regarding reform of the education system.

Faced with the crisis in education, the National Council on Educational Reform (NCER) was established in March 2000 as the Japanese prime minister's advisory board to discuss the direction of educational reform together with various Ministry of Education bodies. While it is natural that education be recognized as a matter of utmost national importance, reform must not be conducted piecemeal by merely looking for remedies for specific problems but should be carried out with a long-term perspective. Since education is inextricably interrelated with society, the process of responding to changing times naturally may entail a degree of trial and error. Frequently, however, the orientation of reform has been strongly affected by the political current of the time or has consisted of myopic countermeasures that are simply reactions to changes in the immediate environment.

This was a problem in prewar Japan, as well. In *Soka kyoiku-gaku taikei* (The System of Value-Creating Pedagogy), which was published in 1930, Makiguchi indicated:

> As is the difficulty with any old, long-established edifice, our thoroughly inconsistent educational system

has been patched up with an endless succession of
stopgap remedial measures. Our schools are unable
to respond to the demands of the new era and, as
a result, are misdirecting the future progress of the
young people who enter them. This is a truly distressing situation.[8]

Challenging the myopic and superficial nature of contemporary Japanese attempts at educational reform, he proposed
that two new institutions be established to develop an educational vision for a new era, namely, an "educational headquarters" to act as an independent, permanent central agency for
education and a "national institute for educational research"
to assist it. The latter was indeed founded soon after the war,
but a deliberative body such as he envisaged has yet to be
established.

The NCER could potentially fulfill this function, but as this
is an ad hoc body, there would be the risk that this important
issue might come to be treated in a stopgap way. This is why I
would like to propose the establishment of a permanent central commission for education committed to the long-term
reconstruction of the entire framework of the educational system. This should be launched as an independent body that is
institutionally insulated from all political influence. Ensuring
independence is indispensable as a means to prevent a loss of
continuity in educational policies in the event of changes in
the administration and also to avoid arbitrary reforms caused
by political interference.

I have in the past called for the principle of the separa-
tion of powers to be expanded to give education a status and
independence coequal to that accorded the executive, legislative, and judicial branches of government. Because edu-

cation is a profound endeavor that shapes the individuals of
future generations, it should be completely independent of
political interference. This also was the spirit of Makiguchi
and his close associate and successor, Josei Toda, who both
campaigned selflessly during the 1920s and 1930s against the
nationalistic education that was pushing Japan on the path
toward war.

Such a permanent central commission should then take
the lead in setting forth firm principles and long-term direc-
tions for reform in education while communicating with
organizations such as the National Institute for Educational
Research of Japan. In addition to this vital mission, this permanent central commission would have a broader focus that
could enable Japan to open a new path toward international
contribution. International exchange and cooperation in the
educational arena, transcending national interests, will serve
as a foundation for world peace. For this reason, I have been
promoting a vision, conceived more than twenty years ago,
for what might be called a "United Nations of Education" to
work toward making education independent of political interference throughout the world. If Japan could take on the role
of promoting the independence of education throughout the
world by establishing a permanent educational commission in
this way, this would doubtless help create a new identity for
Japan as a country devoted to education.

In April 2000, Japan sponsored the first G8 Education Summit, attended by education ministers. I would like to propose
that Japan actively support the regular holding of international educational summits in the future, promoting a broad
range of exchanges not only at the governmental level but
also between individuals actually engaged in education. As
confirmed at the G8 Education Summit, educational issues

are not limited to individual countries. Hence Japan should assume a pivotal role in leading other countries toward international cooperation to open a new horizon for education in the twenty-first century.

Next, I would like to mention some points pertaining to reform of education in schools, which has recently become a focal issue in Japan. The core of this reform has been structural deregulation. The intention is that liberalization in the field of education will be promoted by abolishing the exams between junior and senior high schools in the public school system and introducing greater choice of school. The reforms also include a reduction in overall class hours, aiming to provide more latitude for children's growth by introducing a five-day school week. These measures are presumably a result of recognizing the importance of encouraging competition among schools and in reaction against rote learning. In the Japanese context, if these reforms are enacted without completely thinking them through and providing the resources to ensure they work, we may end up asking too much of children's self-motivation. Makiguchi described the impact that the indiscriminate advocacy of "freedom" can have on the educational process:

> Mere liberation, unaccompanied by a creative, constructive element, falls into directionless indulgence. When one thinks of the impact on the educational economy of the innocent pupils, it is impossible to regard this with indifference.[9]

This warning from the past should not be neglected today. Our communities, our schools, and families need thorough, prudent preparation. As Makiguchi emphasized, methodological reforms must be preceded by unambiguously defining the purpose of education in terms of the happiness of students. Institutional changes that are not guided by clearly defined goals and principles could easily backfire as they have done in the past.

One of Makiguchi's proposals was for a half-day school system, which would of course reduce the amount of time spent at school similar to current discussions. His motivation, however, was not merely his opposition to the overemphasis on rote learning, as is the case at present. His key desire was to promote spiritually and physically balanced growth, whereby children could experience simultaneously the enrichment derived from learning at school and that derived from practical experience in society.

Makiguchi stressed:

> The malady of contemporary education is not so much that there is an overemphasis on factual knowledge, but that educators' approach to the concept of intellectual education is not appropriate. . . . Future education should not disregard or reduce intellectual training but should increase it; it must be thoroughly improved.[10]

He called for a comprehensive change in Japanese attitudes toward education, shifting from an emphasis on factual knowledge alone to the development of intellect and wisdom. He felt that this is the challenge that should be addressed by schools.

Rather than focusing critically on the existing school system, curtailing its functions in such a way as to attack its very foundations, I believe that we should seek a process of reform from the standpoint of restoring our schools' fundamental function as forums for imparting intellectual education in the true sense of the phrase.

Creativity and Experimentation

If we are to truly change school education, empowerment of teachers must be a component. I would like to propose a transition to a more decentralized approach, one that gives each school a freer hand and gives more authority to principals through democratization and transparency in the appointment process, as well as encouraging the creativity and ingenuity of teachers. Because reforms have in the past been imposed uniformly, I believe it has been difficult for teachers to formulate new ideas as various restrictions lead them merely to perform their part adequately and no more.

Education should be for the sake of children and should not be under the monopolistic control of the government. In Japan, the government is deeply involved with details such as screening of textbooks and imposition of the curriculum, which means that we have not cultivated the means to nurture autonomy of schools and teachers or the individuality and creativity of children. Uniform standards should be limited to matters of basic framework, and the independence of the school should be respected in practical matters. At the same time, teachers should encourage one another to enhance the quality of education through a process of trial and error.

In recent discussions on reform, there has been an ongoing debate about the quality of individual teachers, including suggestions that teaching certificates be subject to periodic renewal. What is really needed, however, is for the entire school to unite behind the challenge of enhancing the quality of education across the board. An example of this might be to have all teachers regularly open their classes to observation by their peers, as well as promoting exchanges between teachers of other subjects and from other neighborhood schools for the purpose of research.

The traditional Japanese system is reaching its limits, as seen in the breakdown of the lifetime employment and "promotion by seniority" systems in our companies. Positive competition is required if we are to reinvigorate our society. To enrich school education, teachers need mutual inspiration and motivation, encouragement and solidarity. Moreover, regular open days for children's families and members of the community as well as exchanges of views between elementary, junior, and senior high school teachers in the same community would be useful in deepening cooperation.

In this context, I would like to propose that new and different types of schools be officially accredited and "experimental classes" be promoted. Genuine, internal transformation of school education in Japan requires a more decentralized approach and the encouragement of the creative energy of educators.

Other countries recognize a variety of schools operating under differing educational approaches: Steiner schools grounded in a unique educational philosophy, charter schools in the US, and "free schools" that enable children to select their own subjects of interest. Japan needs to have a similar diversity of schools, a fact that many people now recognize. The NCER is deliberating the question of authorizing community schools, a new type of public school established and operated by the community. This is certainly a worthwhile avenue to consider. To enable creative ideas to be put into practice, I would like to propose that the criteria for approving new types of schools be relaxed. We also need to encourage experimental classes within the existing system and find ways to disseminate information about innovative measures that have been successfully tried out.

Faced with the problems of bullying, violence, and absenteeism, the Soka Gakkai's education division has compiled a collection of records of the practical steps its members have taken as teachers to solve problems. This project has been carried out in response to the proposal on education I made in 1984. I was tremendously gratified to hear recently that more than ten thousand such experiences have been compiled, evidence of the painstaking efforts of the teachers over the years. These are precious records and reports on educational methodologies as put into practice in the field and are an extremely beneficial means of sharing teachers' experiences. Amid growing concern about the flight from learning, it is now the vital role of education to strive to create the kinds of schools where children can always find the joys of learning and living.

This year, Japan's Ministry of Education initiated a policy whereby a school can apply to become a "research development school" with the freedom to determine its own curriculum. The system is open to both public and private schools, and the government will provide financial support. I welcome this system in that it encourages creativity and imagination in the classroom. I also believe that analysis of accumulated results and sharing of information will benefit the educational system as a whole.

Interaction between theory and concrete results from experimentation is a prerequisite, and a good example of this is in the work of the American philosopher John Dewey

(1859–1952), who enhanced and deepened his educational theories through experience gained at the Chicago Laboratory School. In the same way, Makiguchi's *The System of Value-Creating Pedagogy* and Toda's *Suirishiki shido sanjutsu* (A Deductive Guide to Arithmetic) were both based on actual practice in the classroom.

Toda, Makiguchi's most loyal supporter and my own mentor, established a private academy, the Jishu Gakkan, in 1923 as a place to verify through experimentation the theory of value-creating education. Makiguchi referred to the Jishu Gakkan as a materialization of his own vision for elementary schools, describing it as the greatest verification of his work. Meanwhile, determined to continue Toda's work, I have founded a system of schools from the kindergarten to university and postgraduate levels based on Makiguchi's principles of value-creating education.

In addition to establishing a creative learning environment, it is equally important to cultivate humanism in our children through actual experience in society. One well-documented tendency in modern children is egoistic behavior and attenuated human relationships, while the intensely competitive examination system becomes the sole focus of children's lives. In addition, many are so absorbed in the virtual world of the internet, television, and video games that they have become numb to the stimulations offered by the real world.

How can we encourage children to directly communicate with society and nature? One popular idea is involvement in volunteer activities. I believe this should be promoted—not merely through occasional field trips but as continuous ongoing engagement. There should be activities that produce tangible results—work within the community, such as recycling, that contributes to society and provides a sense of fulfillment, as well as planting trees and flowers and other conservation activities.

Recently, children have been becoming more and more violent, and the incidence of juvenile crime is rising. Involvement in constructive, creative activities would lead to the well-balanced physical and spiritual growth of children. After engaging in constructive activities and projects, children would return with healthier emotions and peace of mind, bearing out the words of the American philosopher William James (1842–1910) when he spoke of the need for a "moral equivalent of war"[11] to develop discipline and channel aggression.

In this regard, Makiguchi asserted that, through his vision of a half-day school system, the surplus energy of young people, often directed to antisocial targets, can be used in a way that is of value to society, thus contributing toward both individual happiness and the community at the same time. Experiencing the feeling that one's actions are of use to others gives confidence to young people and becomes a firm foundation for spiritual growth.

The year 2001 has been designated as the UN International Year of Volunteers. Taking this as an opportunity, we should deepen appreciation of volunteer activities throughout society, not just in the limited environment of the school, and pave a path toward a humanitarian society in the twenty-first century.

University Reform

Next, I would like to touch upon the university entrance-examination system, which is a pivotal issue in educational reform in Japan. Currently, as the already excessive pressure of examinations intensifies, one serious problem is the tendency to turn high schools into nothing more than a preparatory stage for entrance to universities. Now that family size is decreasing and the pressure for access to higher education is reduced, Japanese society is presented with a good opportunity to review this system and renew it so it can become truly beneficial to both students and colleges.

What needs to be considered first is diversification of admission processes. I feel there is a need to improve the current university entrance system from a selective screening exam to an aptitude test. The method of university admission should not be limited to written entrance examinations. Broader opportunities should be opened up through diversified processes, such as admission on grounds of special talents and merit. All these efforts should respect and encourage the applicant's will to learn.

The beginning of the university academic year should also be moved from April to September (currently, the academic year in Japan commences in April), both to facilitate smooth transition for exchange students and those returning from studies overseas as well as to provide graduates of Japanese high schools time between graduation and university entrance to engage in a variety of other activities. This period could be used as an opportunity to acquire experience in society, read extensively, or think carefully about their future.

There is also a need to reconsider our approach to university education in terms of both specialization and the provision of a well-rounded general education. In a rapidly changing society, academic disciplines are likely to become further subdivided and highly specialized, reducing the weight of basic liberal arts subjects in college curricula. This will limit the breadth of education a student can receive. Liberal arts at Japanese universities are currently lacking a clear-cut goal or principle, and I would therefore like to call for a reevaluation of our approach in this crucial area. Simultaneously, we must expand education in specialized fields and ensure coordination with the courses offered at graduate school.

It is vital that we define the ideal direction for human education and create a new current of education for the twenty-first century. Soka University of America, Aliso Viejo, will open in 2001 as a liberal arts college focused on providing a well-rounded general education while preparing students to pursue more specialized courses of study, including postgraduate courses. As its founder, I am committed to bold experimentation and full implementation of the ideals of value-creating education.

In all areas of university education, but especially liberal arts, we need to end the tight demarcations among departments and adopt an organic and interdisciplinary approach. For this purpose, faculty members should be urged to drastically reform their teaching methods. One reason why many students find classes unattractive is their outdated content, which is repeated year after year. I have already referred to the dysfunction of the school education system: the problems faced by universities in this regard have also been neglected.

In their interim report, the University Council of the Japanese Ministry of Education emphasized the need to enhance the teaching abilities of faculty members. To prevent the overall quality of university education from being damaged, faculty members must make ceaseless efforts to improve the quality of classes and avoid inertia.

In Japan, Soka University established a Center for Excellence in Teaching and Learning in 2000. The center will support the faculty in various projects to develop innovative teaching methods and also provide students with learning assistance to help them gain the ability to resolve difficulties on their own. At Soka University of America, time will be allocated to critically reflect upon the relationships between the environment and society and our individual lives through a series of courses that comprise the core curriculum.

In this way, rather than merely increasing the hours allocated to general courses, I think it is vital that liberal arts education be positioned as a pillar of the first half of the undergraduate program. The function of liberal arts education is to provide a holistic approach to all academic disciplines, ensuring that the human being is the common ground upon which they are built. Administration of the latter half of a university's undergraduate program must also be made more flexible, with the introduction of a double-major system and a system that allows compatibility in credits and transfers between schools. This would enable students to move to universities in specialized academic fields.

Students in Japan are inclined to prioritize universities or departments that are easy to enter. If this situation persists, it will never generate positive results for either the students or the universities. To avoid this, universities should cooperate in providing classes in areas that students truly wish to pursue. During their time in university, as students' interests develop, they are likely to wish to change courses to a completely different field, which may require moving to a different university. The current system, however, does not allow the transfer of credits and thus discourages this process.

To respond to this, universities in some parts of Japan are starting to form alliances enabling the transfer of credits.

These are bold, important reforms that will greatly benefit the students. Ideally, universities should allow individual students to study what they want, when they want, and where they want. To achieve this, we need to allow mobility, concentrating on the academic discipline and specialization, not the university. This will form part of the development of a lifelong education system.

Another task that universities should address, I believe, is opening their doors to international exchange. Japan, in particular, urgently needs to promote internationalization in all institutions of higher learning.

Soka University aims to be a new kind of university based on the principles of humanism. For this reason, ever since it was established, it has actively promoted educational exchanges with universities in other countries. It has already signed academic exchange agreements with more than seventy universities. Through such exchanges, many students have acquired the opportunity to study abroad, and regular exchanges of faculty members have been promoted. We are striving toward globalization of the educational environment by enhancing mutual understanding among cultures.

The high standards of American universities compared to Japanese universities is often mentioned here. I am convinced that the wellspring of the vigor of American colleges lies in the country's spiritual climate that respects diversity and freedom and welcomes educators and students of many different nationalities.

In Japan, teaching staff have tended to work abroad only for the sake of career advancement, while students often view overseas study purely in terms of future career opportunities. But from the viewpoint of cultural exchange and enhancement of the quality of education in Japan, we urgently need to find ways to increase the flow of students and faculty coming to Japan. Scholarships will be an important means of supporting students studying abroad as well as encouraging foreign students to study in Japan. Creating a fuller scholarship system will therefore be crucial if Japan is to be a country that places the utmost priority on education.

On the same theme, I want to emphasize the importance of language education, especially English, at an early stage. Even if we make structural preparations for international exchange at the university level, unless we break down the language barrier, the range of exchanges will not expand, and these plans will remain "pie in the sky." Moreover, globalization means that linguistic proficiency is becoming an indispensable ability. Language skills can help bring the world together. Language is a tool that enables us to expand our chances of learning about the lives and values of people throughout the world as well as promoting heart-to-heart exchanges. As one concrete measure, it is important to actively promote English education in elementary schools. This, however, should not consist of just bringing forward junior high school English classes but rather focus on learning conversation skills in an enjoyable environment that also deepens understanding of culture. Naturally, we should not neglect the study of Japanese language, history, and culture as well.

Toward a Century Radiant With the Smiles of Children

Lastly, I would like to once more emphasize the global challenge that faces us: the creation of a human society that serves the essential needs of education. When defined as those activities that foster the talents and character of human beings, "education" is in no way limited to classrooms but is a mission that must be undertaken and realized by human society as a whole. We must now go back to the original purpose of education—children's lifelong happiness—and reflect upon the state of our respective societies and our ways of living.

What kind of world should we build for our children to inherit? At the threshold of a new century, we have a great opportunity to seriously face these issues—and it is an opportunity we must seize.

The UN has designated the first decade of the twenty-first century the International Decade for a Culture of Peace and Nonviolence for the Children of the World. I wholeheartedly welcome this designation since it is a theme I have promoted continuously over the years. UNESCO will be assuming a central role in this campaign, but its success depends on a broad range of popular support and cooperation.

The youth division of the SGI-USA has been engaged in Victory Over Violence (VOV), a movement to educate people about nonviolence, since 1999. This movement is conducted through promoting dialogue to disseminate the spirit of nonviolence. The overarching goal is to transform the tendency to downplay the sanctity of life that became deeply rooted in the minds of children during the twentieth century, the century of war and violence. The VOV movement is developing broadly in American society and receiving support from many human rights organizations, schools, and other educational institutions. Above all, it has become a tremendous source of hope and courage for young people who have suffered the effects of violence.

Like the US, Japan also needs to address this tendency to devalue life. Sensational coverage of tragic incidents pointing at the darkness in children's hearts will do nothing to solve the problem. It is society's values that have become inverted. As adults, we must speak out and take action. The Soka Gakkai has consistently emphasized the promotion of peace education at the grassroots level. In line with the UN international decade, I call upon the Soka Gakkai youth division and the education division to play central and active roles in raising awareness of the culture of peace and nonviolence in Japanese society. I believe that through such engagement we can construct a value-creating society and live truly nonegoistic lives grounded in mutual respect.

Education separated from society can have no vital force; likewise, there is no future for a society that has lost sight of the fact that education is its true mission. Education is not a mere right or obligation. I believe that education in the broadest sense is the mission of every individual. To awaken this awareness throughout society must be the highest priority in all our endeavors.

Finally, I would like to conclude by pledging that I will devote all my energy to creating a century in which children's lives will shine with happiness and the magnificent promise of education will finally be fulfilled.

Humanity in Education

August 24, 1984.

N OT A DAY goes by without serious discussion concerning the lamentable state of our educational system. The problem has reached nationwide proportions. Such phenomena as juvenile delinquency, violence at school, truancy, and widespread lethargy among the young constitute no more than the tip of the iceberg. In spite of the fervent attempts being made both at home and in the schools to deal with it, because of the breadth of the issue, so far no solution has been found.

As one person earnestly desiring the wholesome growth and development of youth, I cannot help but be anxious. Since I am not a specialist in the field, I have no intention of discussing individual educational methods or the various aspects of the educational system that require reform. All of these things must be handled with wisdom and in the light of world trends and the situation in Japan. Avoiding hastiness, qualified people must approach these problems, remaining fully aware that cultivating today's youth will determine the fate of tomorrow's Japan.

Restoring Humanity to Education

Politics, however, must not be allowed to take the lead in educational reforms. In all ages, the political authorities have tended to subjugate education and everything else to their own purposes, as was vividly illustrated by modern Japanese education after the establishment, in 1872, of a system dominated by political aims and giving first priority to the achievement of nationalist goals. Slogans such as "increase production and promote industry" and "enrich the country and strengthen the military" were hoisted aloft like imperial banners to which education was obliged to give service. Though this policy may have been partly justified on the basis of the desire to catch up with the Western powers, we must not avert our eyes from the loss it entailed.

Nor can it be said that the constitution and the Fundamental Law of Education adopted after World War II succeeded in avoiding the same pitfalls since, generally speaking, politics again took the lead in the postwar democratic education system. Education was once again called on to serve nationalistic aims, with the difference that postwar efforts to become a great economic power replaced prewar and wartime efforts to become a great military power. Under such circumstances, when the national aim collapses, educational aims are left dangling in the air. It is therefore by no means coincidental that the dark cloud of educational devastation that engulfed our country from the 1970s into the 1980s coincided with frustrations resulting from the end of Japan's era of high-pace economic growth.

The true goal of education should be the cultivation of individual character on the basis of respect for humanity. We must admit, however, that in modern Japan education has been used as a means for cultivating people to be of value to the nation and big business; that is, people who will function effectively within the national and economic structure. For some time, I have advocated the establishment of a fourth branch of government—that of education—independent of the present three branches—legislative, executive, and judiciary—as a method of dealing with the ills and distortions created by education being dominated by politics. What has been lost in the modern Japanese system of education, led as it has been since the late nineteenth century by political considerations, is humanity.

On the basis of his many years of practice and study in teaching, Tsunesaburo Makiguchi (1871–1944) defined education concisely and clearly in the following way: the goal of education must not be set by scholars and must not be taken advantage of by other parties. The goal of education must be one with the goal of life. And this means that it must enable students to attain a life of happiness.

Putting to good use his more than thirty years of experience in practical education and adding to that his astute observations of society, Makiguchi developed a definition of happiness in the form of his original theory of value. He could achieve this because, throughout his life, he kept an enlightened eye turned always on humanity.

In this connection, I am always deeply moved by a passage from the writings of Victor Hugo (1802–85), the great romanticist who devoted himself to establishing the autonomy of education, to relieving poverty, and to ensuring freedom for all: "Light makes whole. Light enlightens. All the generous sunrays of society spring from science, letters, the arts, and education. Make men, make men."[1]

But I do not think we need Hugo's words to realize that the main significance of education is to "make men." It is essential that future educational reforms must be made for the sake of humanity, not politics. I further insist that nostalgia for the nationalistic Japanese education of the past—which is on the rise these days—is stimulated by doubt concerning the situation of the present and represents that refusal to learn from history.

The question of how to develop educational reforms that are rooted in considerations of humanity has been argued, and studies and proposals have been made from many different angles. With that in mind, instead of going into structural reforms, I would like to offer some thoughts on the foundational principles that should guide these reforms, with an emphasis on three aspects: totality, creativity, and internationalism.

Totality of Wisdom

When I speak of totality I mean interrelation. No thing or event exists in isolation; everything is interrelated in some way with everything else to produce one great total image. To take an immediately apparent example, I might cite the human body itself in which the head, hands, torso, legs, internal organs, and all individual cells are intimately intermeshed to form the whole. And we cannot overlook the connection between the physical and spiritual. Modern depth psychology and ecology show that interrelations expand infinitely to connect human beings with one another, with the world of nature, and with the entire universe. Inseparably bound, the microcosm and the macrocosm work together in wondrous rhythm.

In the words of Goethe's (1749–1832) *Faust:*

Lo, single things inwoven, made to blend,
To work in oneness with the whole, and live.[2]

From ancient times, the ability to perceive the invisible threads interweaving all things has been considered a kind of wisdom. But modern civilization has turned its back on this wisdom and has pursued instead a continual course of fragmentation. Though perhaps an inevitable part of the development of human knowledge, this tendency, while producing noteworthy results in the physical realm, has created a condition in which the cords that once connected individual to individual, to say nothing of the individual and nature, have been severed; and individuals groan in the small, enclosed, and lonely spaces to which they have been driven.

In terms of learning and education, this state of affairs can be compared to the way in which humankind has ignored the totality of wisdom and instead has allowed the departmentalization of learning to exist for its own sake. Unrelated to the values of human happiness and a better way of life, learning goes its own way, reaching ever-higher proportions.

The great educator Yukichi Fukuzawa (1835–1901), who lived in the latter half of the nineteenth century when modernization was the central issue in Japan, saw this from a very early date. He once remarked: "This informed person is informed about things but not about the connections among them and is ignorant of the principle mutually connecting this and that. Learning consists solely in understanding mutual relations among things. Learning that does not take such relations into consideration serves no useful purpose."[3] Further, he observed: "The informed person who does not know connections among things differs from a dictionary only in that he eats and the dictionary does not."[4]

In other words, the person who, like a dictionary, is a compendium of unrelated information knows much but ignores interrelations and is therefore useless and nonconstructive.

Of course, Fukuzawa, the author of *Gakumon no susume* (*An Encouragement of Learning*), who studied widely himself and stimulated others to do the same, is not attacking learning, but only learning and knowledge for their own sakes. Nor do I think his words reflect pragmatism and practicality alone.

Fukuzawa speaks of connections among things (the Japanese word *en*, which he uses in this meaning, is found in such core Buddhist terms as *engi*, the pivotal doctrine of dependent origination). Determining what connection study and learning have with oneself—that is, what meaning they have—represents an inclination toward the kind of totality of which I have been speaking. This same inclination can be seen in the philosophy of Henri Bergson (1859–1941), who made the famous statement, "Living comes first of all."[5]

Undeniably, the pursuit of learning for learning's sake has been a great driving force in the development of modern science. However, when the end results include nuclear weapons and environmental pollution, we are compelled to examine the social responsibility of scientists. Scientists must ask themselves what connection their learning has with their own fate and with that of all humankind.

On the more practical plane of actual education, I often hear of students who no longer read great classics and literary masterpieces but content themselves with digests providing all the information they need to pass literature examinations. They know no more than the digests tell them and have no desire to learn further. Even in this age of audiovisual technology and mass media, this is cause for concern.

Information learned from a digest for nothing but the purpose of passing an examination is nothing but knowledge for knowledge's sake. Reading great literature is an opportunity to make connections with the spirits of outstanding writers and in this way to improve and broaden one's self toward further development. Such spiritual improvement comes only from direct contact and cannot be obtained through digests. Although it may be possible to obtain much superficial information without going through the labor of actually reading great books, people who choose this path become spiritually shallow and biased.

This applies equally in all branches of learning, not just literature: educators and students alike must make unceasing and diligent efforts to establish connections between compartmentalized learning and the totality of wisdom. Obviously, abuses in the educational system—like excessive emphasis on examinations—must be corrected. But even if the system remains imperfect, as long as such efforts are made, students will become people of sufficient ability to transcend its faults. They will go beyond petty egoistic thinking to become total human beings who, while considering the whole of wisdom, relate their own lives to the fate of all humankind. I am firmly convinced that cultivating excellent human beings of this caliber is the true purpose of education.

Creativity: Badge of Humanity

Creativity could be called the badge, or proof, of our humanity. Human beings are the only creatures capable of striving for higher goals on their own volition, dynamically creating new value with each passing day.

Creativity is the womb from which individuality blossoms. All humans are different; each has a unique personality. But often the personality withers in the bud, before it has a chance to come to full flower. In different terms, before coming into individual radiance, personalities frequently freeze at the stage characterized by mere idiosyncrasies. Creativity is a stimulus operating from within to thaw this imbalance and allow the personality to grow and bloom more fully. Buddhism describes the flowering of the personality that emanates from the depths of life with the statement that each person's individuality is as unique as cherry, plum, peach, or damson blossoms.

Accordingly, creativity is a brilliant force rising spontaneously from within. This is what Alfred North Whitehead (1861–1947) had in mind when, addressing a group of English students about to leave school in the devastation following World War I, he said that they had all the essential sources of growth within themselves.[6] Knowledge can be obtained from without, but creativity and imagination must be activated from within. Sadly, schools and other institutions of learning today seem to me to fail in stimulating and cultivating creativity.

Young people may be oriented toward good or evil. It is of primary importance for people concerned with education on the broader scale to believe in the creativity of each young person with whom they come in contact, cultivate it warmly, and persistently endeavor to enable it to bloom brilliantly.

I do not deny that abuses in the system—like being absorbed in acquiring the methods to pass examinations—constitute a great barrier to improvement. But it would be irresponsible to lay all the blame at the system's door, because exchanges between human beings are the soil in which creativity grows. Creative vitality gushes forth like a fountain as a consequence of spiritual exchanges—sometimes severe, sometimes warm— between human beings who share complete trust given with no thought of reward.

In this connection, I am vividly reminded of a passage in the famous "Letters" of Plato (c. 428–c. 348 BCE). Regarding people who claimed to know that which he himself had seriously studied, whether as students of his or of other teachers or from their own discoveries, Plato said: "

> Such writers can in my opinion have no real acquaintance with the subject. I certainly have composed no work in regard to it, nor shall I ever do so in future, for there is no way of putting it in words like other studies. Acquaintance with it must come rather after a long period of attendance on instruction in the subject itself and of close companionship, when, suddenly, like a blaze kindled by a leaping spark, it is generated in the soul and at once becomes self-sustaining.[7]

In this extremely acute comment, the "subject" to which Plato refers is no doubt the quintessence of his own philosophy projected against the background of what he learned under his great teacher, Socrates. It is equally certain that what he was trying to describe is of a lofty spiritual nature.

His statement that "like a blaze kindled by a leaping spark, it is generated in the soul and at once becomes self-sustaining" is an idea widely applicable to modern education. Recognizing each student as a unique personality and transmitting something through contacts between that personality and the personality of the instructor is more than a way of implanting knowledge: it is the essence of education.

In certain parts of Japan, child education is called *koyarai,* a term that means allowing the child to stand on their own, out in front, while the parent or educator pushes them from behind. In the words of a Japanese folklorist, this is exactly the opposite of the modern educational tendency to stand in front of the child and attempt to pull them forward. The *koyarai* philosophy has something important to say to contemporary educational thought, which considers children less than complete, or mature, human beings until they have completed a prescribed curriculum. Recognition in the field of anthropology of the three elements that modern civilization has overlooked—the primitive, the subconscious, and the childlike—is called a great discovery of the twentieth century. Undeniably, education today stands at a turning point in relation to discovering children in the sense of attempting to learn ways to recognize and appreciate the individual personalities of young people.

Educators must make the effort to call forth the creative powers latent in their students. In this undertaking, they require endurance, courage and, affection. To cultivate others, an educator must have a glowing, appealing personality. Socrates's power to move others was compared to the shock of a sting ray. When told this, Socrates replied, "As for myself, if the sting ray paralyzes others only through being paralyzed itself, then the comparison is just, but not otherwise."[8]

Similarly, teachers must be constantly creative if they are to evoke creativity from their students. If teachers are not, all their talk of creativity will remain nothing but empty words.

There is nothing wrong with keeping in step with advances in the computer age by introducing all kinds of new equipment to make education more convenient and efficient. But no amount of equipment compensates for the absence of those old, but forever new, virtues of effort, endurance, courage, and affection. Should these virtues, together with the essential creative vitality, dry up, the outlook will become grave; relying on the latest technology to alleviate it is to put the cart before the horse.

International Outlook

The third element is internationalization. In this age, when the pace of internationalization is accelerating throughout the world, the future of Japan can well be said to depend on the ability to cultivate and foster capable people with truly international perspectives.

For better or worse, Japan has become a world economic leader, and what Japan does has an immense influence on what the world at large does. Dr. Henry Kissinger (1923–), with whom I have met on several occasions, says history offers no reason why an economic superpower will not develop into a military superpower. From my own standpoint, however, no matter what history may have been like, to continue to enjoy peace and prosperity, Japan must follow a course other than militarization. And if that path has never before been trodden, Japan must be courageous and take pride in blazing it.

The path I speak of is that of a nation devoted to culture. As an outcome of my many private endeavors and undertakings, I have come to see clearly that, whereas it may seem modest and inconspicuous, mutual understanding achieved through cultural exchanges is very powerful.

An episode from the Russo-Japanese War of 1904–5 is pertinent to this topic. As the war was drawing to a close, Japan was looking about for a nation to serve as mediator. In strict secrecy the Japanese government dispatched two envoys: Kentaro Kaneko (1853–1942), a government official, to the United States, and Kencho Suematsu (1855–1920), a politician and scholar, to England.

Perhaps because the two men had been classmates at Harvard, Kaneko was able to convince President Theodore

Roosevelt (1858–1919) to assist him. The president, however, asked Kaneko to give him information that would help him explain the Japanese viewpoint to the American people. Kaneko gave Roosevelt a copy of a book, written in English by Inazo Nitobe (1862–1933), called *Bushido: The Soul of Japan*, in which the code of the warrior is explained as the basis of Japanese moral education. The president read the book in an evening, found it convincing, and agreed to serve as mediator between Japan and Russia. Suematsu, on the other hand, attended English salons, where he boasted of Japan as a land as much on the way up as the rising sun and was laughed at. This episode illustrates the powerful influence culture—as spotlighted in Nitobe's book—can exert.

Unfortunately, after the Russo-Japanese War, Japan pursued a headlong course of militarization. And today, we will find ourselves in a very dangerous predicament unless we strive to make culture the base of our economic power.

To achieve this, the most important thing is to educate people so that they are broadly cultivated and have a mastery of languages. Because this is being realized, foreign language education in Japan, which has in the past been criticized as useless, is now, I am happy to say, being reappraised. I want to make it clear, however, that though an essential element, proficiency in other languages alone does not make a person truly international. As I have said, this requires broad cultivation, not only practical expertise in politics and economics but also an understanding of one's own culture and tradition and those of other peoples as well. The kind of cultivation I have in mind must be so deeply ingrained that it manifests itself in behavior and deportment. As T. S. Eliot (1888–1965) asserted, culture is living. It is not a mere surface accretion but is acquired only when it has been bred into a person since the time of childhood training in manners. Consequently, a nation devoted to culture must be a nation devoted to education. The great writer Ogai Mori (1862–1922) once observed:

> I divide modern Japanese scholars into those with one and those with two legs. The new Japan is a whirlpool in which the cultures of the East and the West combine. Some scholars stand in the Eastern one and others in the Western one, but both kinds are one-legged. . . . The age needs scholars with two legs, one planted in each culture. Truly substantive debate is possible only with such people, who are the elements of harmony necessary at the present time.[9]

The problem indicated here by Mori, himself a man of great cultivation in Japanese, Chinese, and Western cultures, remains unresolved to this day. I think we can expand his meaning of *two-legged* to represent not merely knowledge of the cultures of East and West but also wide and well-balanced cultivation in general. Today, as internationalization continues to advance, we are in greater need than the people of Mori's time of such "elements of harmony."

In relation to the need for balance and harmony, I should like to mention something that has recently been on my mind. The attitude of the Japanese people toward their own tradition and the traditions of the rest of the world seems to me to have swung, pendulum-like, too wide and too fast in the last fifty years or so. Before World War II, when we were taught that Japan was a divine nation, total rejection of everything un-Japanese was taken for granted. Since World War II, on the other hand, the Japanese tradition—even the best parts of it—has been despised and ignored. Recently, the pendulum seems to be swinging back in the opposite direction again. If this change of attitude is part of an arrogance born of economic success, I am deeply afraid that it could lead Japan in the wrong direction. Rejection and adoration of the foreign are two sides of the same coin, and both indicate a lack of self-confidence and independence. Vacillation and imbalance are the outcome of a lack of self-confidence. People who persist in such a condition can never be called truly international, no matter how much they may turn their view outward.

Economic and military power can breed arrogance but not self-confidence, which can be fostered only through cultural development. This is why, in Japanese schools, I think it would be a good idea to place more stress on the proper use of the Japanese language and on the study of such aspects of our irreplaceable heritage as great literature and the traditional arts. Without the mature knowledge of one's own language, foreign-language studies cannot produce maximum results. From all that I have seen or heard, people who excel in international contacts are bright and appealing as Japanese personalities. Cultivation in one's own culture as well as in other cultures is what it takes to be truly cosmopolitan; I think our institutions of learning ought to set as one of their goals the development of such internationally minded people.

Although, as I have said, I am no specialist, I have enumerated these three points—totality, creativity, and internationalization—because I think a profound understanding of their importance is essential to the reforms that must be made in our current educational system.

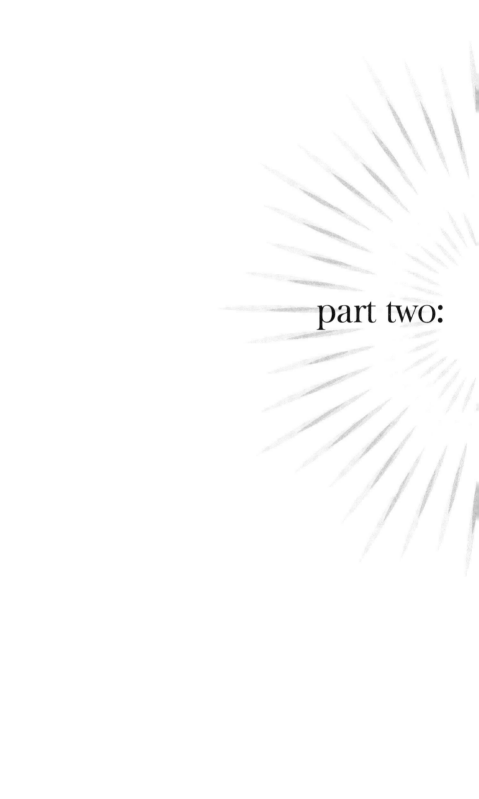

part two:

lectures for students

Be Creative Individuals

Soka University's third entrance ceremony, Tokyo, April 9, 1973.

I WOULD LIKE TO offer my congratulations to every one of you on your admission to Soka University. At the same time, I would like to express my deep appreciation for the wholehearted exertions made during the past two years by the university administrators, professors, and faculty, as well as all the students, to solidify the foundations of this new institution. I would also like to extend my appreciation to the parents and all who have offered their help and encouragement. As the founder, I offer my heartfelt thanks to all those concerned.

This university belongs to all of you. It is yours to shape and create. It must not be an ivory tower isolated from society. Instead, it must be a towering beacon of hope, filled with boundless possibilities for the unfolding of a new era, a new future for humankind. I hope that this university will be a place where the ethos of constantly seeking and striving to find ways to contribute to humanity and society, of working for the happiness of every individual, will never be lost—even in the distant future.

Today, I would like to examine the influence universities have exerted on society from a historical viewpoint. I do not intend to delve into an abstruse, abstract theory of the role of the university. I am not qualified to give such a talk, nor is there any need for one. I intend only to offer a few examples of the ways in which the university—or, on a broader scale, learning in general—has been a driving force in history.

Emergence of the University in the West

All of you are familiar with the Renaissance—the cultural awakening that took place in fourteenth- and fifteenth-century Europe. This was a time when the long-dormant spirit of humanism awakened to inspire a movement that produced—in painting, sculpture, literature, and the other arts—a vast number of great works glorifying and extolling humanity and the human being. This provided the impetus for Europe to greet the dawn of a new era. I am certain I am not the only person who senses in the artistic creations of the Renaissance a joyous celebration of our common humanity. This revolution in art and literature, which constituted an important turning point in European civilization, was not something limited to these fields; nor did it come about by mere chance or happenstance. The way had been prepared by a quickening that arose from the depths of European culture. This may be traced to a revival of learning that had its origins in the Middle Ages, which, though less well known, was in many ways as important as the Renaissance of the fourteenth and fifteenth centuries.

Historians sensitive to its value call this movement the Renaissance of the Twelfth Century, and it was during this period that the European university came into being. In the early Middle Ages, the knowledge people were thought to need consisted of the seven liberal arts—Latin grammar, rhetoric, logic, arithmetic, astronomy, geometry, and music. These were considered necessary to the reading of the Bible—in order to understand the natural law of God—and for the operation of the systems of customary law necessary to maintain the authority of secular monarchs. Arithmetic and astronomy were needed for calculating the church calendar, and music for church rituals; the other branches of learning were applied in law and politics. This was the highest level of education of the day.

In about the twelfth century, to these fields of study were added—especially in Spain and Italy—mathematics, philosophy, geography, and jurisprudence, all of which were imported from the Islamic world. Among these imports were subjects that had been known to the ancient Greeks and Romans but had been lost to the people of medieval Europe. Other elements were brought from India and the East by Muslim and Italian merchants. With the acquisition of this heritage of ancient—though new to Europe—learning, there arose an irrepressible drive to absorb still more, newer knowledge and to accumulate and systematize it. Young people in search of knowledge broke free from the bonds of the existing monastic schools and sought new sites of learning. It might be said that the scholarly vocations arose in response to their demands, with the formation in Paris and Bologna of communities of teachers and students. These communities signaled the emergence of the European university.

The word *university* derives from the Latin *universitas*, one of the meanings of which is an association or guild, a community of people bound by common interests. In other words, the university is originally a community of teachers and students; it is not something that is found in buildings or educational systems but which grows out of connections and bonds among people. The university at Paris originated largely as a venue for the research and reformulation of theology. At the university at Bologna, the greatest interest centered on law and jurisprudence. Both were the outcome of critical reflection on traditional ecclesiasticism and of more modern, rational, and practical forms of learning and knowledge relevant to the new, contractual commercial relations developing at the time. It was humanism and the humanities that provided the spiritual core of this quest for learning. I believe that the growth of the bourgeoisie and the increased vigor of commerce made possible the development of an intellectual class with the university as its pinnacle. These movements, outside the framework of aristocratic dominance and firmly embedded in the humanities, created and cultivated the conditions for the Renaissance.

A careful examination of the human condition, combined with a desire for learning in search of truth, stimulated a revival of the arts, eventually culminating in a stirring paean to humankind. The Renaissance could not have altered the course of history if it had been merely a shallow, essentially rootless movement limited to literature and the arts. It was epoch making because it drew energy from a new awakening of the individual self, freed from the restraints of the old order and profoundly confident of the ability of scholarship to ascertain truth and affirm knowledge.

The work of one of the giants of the Renaissance, Leonardo da Vinci (1452–1519), reveals the extent of the impact of the new learning. The rules of perspective employed in his painting are based on his knowledge of geometry, while his grasp of anatomy gained through actual dissections made possible his precise renderings of the human body and animals. In this way, we can see that it was the long accumulation of learning and knowledge in the years before the Renaissance that made possible the brilliant works of that period. The point I want to make is this: movements that have the power to shape history result from free, untrammeled human thought; they flow from the vital tides of life itself. To flourish, endure, and have wide effect, a civilization needs to be grounded in a profound philosophical heritage. Without such a heritage, a civilization cannot produce geniuses. And, even if it could produce them, such geniuses would find no place to manifest their talents. Conversely, no social structure that rests on the power of coercion can exert a genuine shaping influence on human life or leave a brilliant record of cultural attainment.

People have a tendency to appreciate only the glorious, conspicuous products of history. They copy styles, respect established traditions, and allow these to govern their actions. Yet they often ignore the deeper causes that made possible the achievement of such glories. I believe that the failure to look more deeply into historical phenomena can explain why some movements to reform society in the past miscarried. Efforts that are focused solely on the attainment of immediate goals will ultimately prove futile.

The University as a Basic Current of Civilization

The university is a repository of intellectual heritage. The quality and significance of the research and education carried out there can determine the fate of a nation, a society, or an entire civilization. Where learning flourishes, the people will definitely flourish.

Many ancient civilizations were grounded in a flourishing of learning. The world of Islam also had many centers of learning, as did India in the heyday of Buddhism. The Indian Buddhist university-temple of Nalanda, which ran an area of tens of square kilometers, reached its zenith between the fifth and seventh centuries. Larger in scale than most modern universities and much older than the universities of Europe, Nalanda was a spiritual center for both India and the whole of Asia. Many Chinese students are known to have gone there to study. At one time, Nalanda could have accommodated as many as ten thousand scholar-monks. The Chinese priest Hsüan-tsang (Xuanzang; c. 602–64), who visited Nalanda, recorded his impressions in *Da Tang xiyu ji* (*The Great Tang Dynasty Record of the Western Regions*). Excavations of several study and dormitory rooms have recently established the veracity of these observations. Nalanda developed and propagated the ideas of Mahayana Buddhism for centuries, until it was destroyed by invading Muslim forces.

It is possible to trace the influence of this university in the spiritual culture of the East, especially the great flourishing of Buddhist culture, which spread from India to China and on to Japan. Recalling the thousands of Buddhist priests who once earnestly discussed Buddhism, debated important points, and then put what they had learned into practice in their respective cultural contexts, I am convinced that Nalanda must indeed have been a key source for the spiritual culture of the East that has long commanded the world's admiration.

I sincerely hope that all of you will maintain the confidence that when learning is deepened and developed at the most essential, underlying level, it provides a source of energy and creativity from which a magnificent flourishing of culture proceeds. Please have confident faith in the fact that it is in the profound oceanic currents, rather than the bright surface waves, that real power and value reside. Furthermore, respect for humanity must be the basis of all institutions of learning. I have already discussed how the Renaissance grew out of the humanism that flourished in the early medieval universities, but something similar can also be said of more ancient institutions of learning that cannot accurately be described as universities in the modern sense.

The famous Academy of Plato (c. 428–c. 348 BCE) in the grove of Akademos is a case in point. In the Athens of his time, the Sophists had acquired considerable influence through their rhetoric and their purely pragmatic, if not mercenary, approach to teaching—they imparted to students only such knowledge as was needed to get ahead in the world. The Sophists's approach was opposed by Socrates (c. 470–399 BCE), who upheld the search for truth as the authentic ideal of education. Confronting the decline of the Hellenic world, he sought to reform Athens on the basis of a philosophy devoted to understanding the essence of humanity and human nature. For this reason, he took a stand against philosophers who taught only "realistic" compromise and accommodation with political authority. He devoted himself to the quest for the kind of knowledge whose validity would endure eternally.

For Socrates, the market, the street corner, the evening meal, or any of the places people gathered were opportunities for sharing his convictions with young people and to combat corrupt and compromised teaching practices. He conducted relentless dialogue and, through this, intellectual and spiritual training in what amounted to a university without campus or buildings. Inheriting the philosophical essence of Socrates, Plato established his Academy. Though he employed a fixed locale, the education he conducted there was of the humanistic kind that Socrates had favored. In Plato's day, it was customary in Athens to treat mealtimes as an opportunity for intellectual discussion and debate. Plato made the fullest use of this practice in his school. In addition, he no doubt conducted lively symposiums on subjects of philosophical and universal human concern during strolls with his students.

Dialogue between students and teachers was at the heart of the search for truth conducted by Plato and his followers. It was the pride of the Academy that teacher and student worked together to seek and attain truth. Though entrance requirements were strict, and in this sense it retained an elitist air, the institution rested on a foundation of faith in freedom and a desire to reform and improve society through the study and practice of philosophy. The school may have been open both to young men and women, and it always remained vigilant against any attempts by secular authority to encroach on its academic freedom. Established around 400 BCE and in operation—until it was finally closed by the Roman emperor Justinian (c. 482–565)—for approximately nine centuries, the Academy was a major force in the development of the spiritual and intellectual heritage of the West. It was, in my view, the human focus of the methods adopted at the Academy—collaborative research by teachers and learners and an unwavering commitment to dialogue—that enabled it to continue for so long and to exert such an important influence in history.

The teaching method of Shakyamuni (c. 560–c. 480 BCE), known to the world as the Buddha, is a still older example of a thorough commitment to dialogue. It was through the informal back-and-forth of question and response that Shakyamuni strove to impart to others the essence of his enlightenment about the fundamental laws governing humanity and the cosmos. Almost all of the sutras that record his teachings are written in a dialogue form in which Shakyamuni directly confronts and addresses the nature of human suffering and reveals the truth of his own enlightenment. In later times, vast bodies of Buddhist doctrinal material were compiled and systematized, but it must always be borne in mind that human interaction committed to refinement of character and the search for truth lies at the basis of it all.

The European Renaissance impulse to return to the learning and methods of ancient Greece reveals but one manifestation of the enormous influence of Plato's Academy. In like manner, Shakyamuni's teachings have left an imprint on virtually all of Eastern history. I believe that the power to exert such an influence stems ultimately from making humanity the focus of all endeavors in the quest for truth. Both traditions are animated by the determination to reveal and explain the essence of our humanity, to encourage and awaken the most noble and elevated aspects of human nature. Any learning or search for truth not rooted in a concern for humanity is doomed to be abstract, futile, shallow, and fruitless. At present the world stands in danger once again of losing sight of this essential focus on humanity.

It is my hope that all of you will continue to pursue the path of scholarship and learning with a firm sense of pride in the mission of such a pursuit of truth: to demonstrate and open the way forward toward a better, more humane future, one in which humanity is revived and restored to its rightful place.

Increased Spiritual Freedom

Having shared with you my views on the original purpose of the university, I wish to make the following request: that you always strive to be creative individuals.

The "Soka" in Soka University means value creation. This in turn means that the basic aim of our university must be to create the kind of value needed by society for it to become a healthier and more wholesome place. This is the kind of value that must be offered—or returned—to society. Consequently, all students here should cultivate their creative abilities in the effort to provide a rich vision for the future and contribute in a meaningful way to society.

Creativity is much more than simply having the occasional good idea. Of course, even to come up with such ideas requires a firm foundation of basic knowledge. And creative work in the fields of scholarship and learning is incomparably more demanding. It is like a mountain peak: it cannot exist without a broad base of knowledge and a solid foundation of deep thinking and reflection. The university is the most suitable place to establish such a foundation. Unfortunately, although most universities in Japan today are blessed with the necessary conditions to do this, there is a distressing lack of will to direct learning toward the ultimate goal of creative activity—they fail to serve as venues for the development of genuinely creative personalities. I want Soka University to be different. I want it to become an institution brimming with creative vitality, and I want it to introduce fresh currents into society.

The cultivation of creativity must be rooted in the soil of a rich spirituality. This in turn points to the vital importance of maintaining spiritual freedom. Independent thought and creative work are impossible when the human spirit is subjected to restraining or distorting pressures. Inexhaustible fonts of creative thinking can be tapped only where mind and spirit can roam freely, exploring all perspectives and possibilities. The various historical examples I have mentioned were universities in which the spirit was given just such free rein.

But spiritual freedom does not mean spiritual license. It does not mean thinking and acting in a willful, arbitrary manner. True development can take place only in the presence of both expansive liberty and a high degree of self-discipline.

In my view this means the opportunity to grow by sharing ideas through dialogue, provoking and catalyzing each other toward an expanded field of vision and ultimately to profound and encompassing insight into the nature of things. Both in Plato's Academy and in the ancient Buddhist university at Nalanda there was freedom; but there was also stern confrontation with truth. Thus there was creative, original thinking. And it was precisely for this reason that the Academy and Nalanda were able to bequeath such rich spiritual heritages to their respective spheres of civilization.

Evidence of the fact that strict training is integral to any effort to expand spiritual freedom can also be seen in the less ancient examples of Oxford and Cambridge. In both universities, where many seminal scholars have been trained and much enduring research produced, an educational system is followed whose rigors reflect the universities' medieval roots. At the same time, students are afforded the high degree of freedom required to grow spiritually and to prepare themselves to make their contributions to society.

What is the source of the energy that enables individuals to extend the scope of their spiritual freedom and expand the scale of their being? To answer this question, we must inevitably return to the more fundamental issue of the nature of the human being. We must engage in a quest for the kind of philosophy that brings forth, develops, and elevates latent human talents, resolving the myriad contradictions of the human condition and bringing these to a higher, more creative synthesis. All the educational institutions I have mentioned have been built on this kind of philosophical bedrock. The untrammeled development of learning and rich cultural flowering have always arisen from the earnest effort to apprehend the nature of life and humanity and to unleash people's inherent potentialities. Here, I am convinced, is found the key to creativity.

I hope Soka University will always seek to bring the study and understanding of humanity to completion and perfection. Based on this, I hope the university will produce an authentic flowering of scholarly achievement. I want all of you to advance in your studies and in the search for truth, always rooted in this consistent effort to build and develop your humanity, so that you can become the driving force for the transformation of society. I urge you to be creative individuals worthy of the name of Soka University: Please take this as your motto, your distinction, your character. If such habits of the heart and mind can become firmly established as the university's noble tradition, I am convinced that Soka University will play an important, invigorating role in the world of Japanese university education, which now seeks desperately for a sense of direction.

Pride and Devotion

To change the subject slightly, it is my honor to have shared enthusiastic discussions with the famous British historian Arnold J. Toynbee (1889–1975) on a wide range of topics, including history, philosophy, art, science, and education. At our first meeting, I was surprised by the way Professor Toynbee and his wife, Veronica, greeted me. He expressed his gratitude to me for visiting his alma mater, Oxford; Mrs. Toynbee (1893–1980) for visiting her alma mater, Cambridge. It is true that I visited England at the invitation of both these universities; but I had not expected that these would be the first words I would hear from Professor and Mrs. Toynbee. Their words, however, showed me just how much pride and devotion they felt toward Oxford and Cambridge.

In Japan, state universities are considered more prestigious than private ones; but in Europe and the United States, the opposite is often the case, as is illustrated by Oxford, Cambridge, and Harvard, all of which were founded as nonstate institutions. The graduates of such schools are typically very proud of and devoted to their alma mater. When they succeed in their careers, they contribute sizable sums to their universities, which are thereby enabled to improve facilities and services. Please do not worry; I am not saying that you must become successful so that you can make contributions to Soka University!

Even though as institutions of learning they have a public aspect, private universities are more independent of national authority. Fundamentally, they are founded to train people and make academic advances toward realizing a unique set of ideals or guiding vision. Being autonomous, private universities are the product of the actions of all the people who operate and study at them. This is what distinguishes them from universities founded or run by national or local governments. As I have stressed, the very concept of the university began with such private associations. As an institution, the university emerged spontaneously and was not created to be the servant of governmental needs.

I want all of you to play your parts in building Soka University and bringing it to an ever-higher degree of completion. Do not think of your education here as the mere accumulation of learning. Do not regard the university as a passport to a good job. While you are here, engage in lively dialogues with your teachers and help evolve a university that is vibrant and warm. You have much to do in this process of creation and construction, since Soka University is new and its academic traditions are not yet firmly established. I shall be observing what you do and shall always be ready to offer whatever assistance I can.

I earnestly hope that not only during your time as students but also after graduation you will take pride in this institution, watch over it, and offer it as much support as possible. Since you have just entered the university, perhaps I am being a bit hasty in talking about things that will take place only after graduation, but it is my strong desire that you will care for, take pride in, and warmly support your alma mater, in whatever position or place you may find yourselves in the future. Just as Professor Toynbee feels the greatest pleasure to hear his alma mater admired, I too hope that you will become people who can take the greatest pride in this university, which is to be developed by your own efforts, and feel gratitude toward those who appreciate it. As founder, this would give me the greatest pleasure.

A Modern Renaissance

Contemporary civilization has reached a turning point, summed up in the stark question: Can humanity survive? The threat to peace posed by the arms race and a blind faith in progress seem to be propelling humanity on a veritable death march. What should we do—what can we do—to enable humankind to survive? Enlightened scholars now debate this issue passionately.

I wish to urge that what we need in such times as these is a true restoration of humanity. By this I am not supporting a shallow anthropocentrism or faith in human omnipotence.

The revival or restoration I have in mind must enable human beings to live in harmony with all of our fellow living creatures. People must cease being the servants of machines and become once more masters of our own technological creations. The renaissance I have in mind would help us find a way to achieve this. This renaissance must begin with a revival in the fields of philosophy and learning. If humanity can rouse and sate a new enthusiasm for learning and the pursuit of truth, if we can turn our wide-open eyes to the future, I am certain that the kind of philosophy needed to enable human survival will be elucidated and established. Such a philosophy will not only contribute to the survival of humanity—the first sine qua non of education—but will also underpin a new civilization that will truly celebrate humanity. Soka University will have fulfilled its purpose if it can contribute in a meaningful way to the attainment of this enormous goal.

The task of creating such a university is clearly not an easy one. It demands perseverance as well as repeated, rigorous debate and sustained determination. Results may not be immediately apparent. But if all the people associated with Soka University now and in the future—comrades sharing the same aspiration—can develop an organic collaborative unity, even such great dreams can be achieved.

Please enjoy a rich, full student life, not only as representatives of this institution but also as its proud founders and constructors. Let your experiences here serve as a springboard to a fulfilled and satisfying life after graduation.

From here on, education will be my central work and preoccupation. How can humanity of the twenty-first century find peace and happiness—this is my sole concern. It is from this perspective that I ask you to accept responsibility for the future of humankind.

From the bottom of my heart, I ask the members of the faculty to do all within their power to help our students grow into fine human beings. I shall conclude my remarks by expressing my hope for and pride in the part that Soka University will play in the future of humanity.

The Flowering of Creative Life Force

Soka University's fourth entrance ceremony,
Tokyo, April 18, 1974.

TODAY I WILL offer not so much a lecture as some words of greeting. Having just returned from a trip abroad, I am not yet fully adjusted to the time change, and I must ask your forgiveness if I jump from one subject to another or fail to make myself clear.

First of all, I want to express to you my heartfelt felicitations on your splendid triumph over the difficulties posed by the entrance examinations. Your successful entrance into this university is truly an occasion for rejoicing. As you know, knowledge and learning are not of themselves good or evil. After having spent four years studying here, you will be equipped either to become public-minded intellectuals or to put your talents to destructive, antisocial use. Which you will become depends on how you exercise your free will. It is, however, my fervent hope that during the next four years you will pursue your studies guided by a sense of justice and conscience.

I have just returned from a trip undertaken to promote international goodwill and cultural exchange. I left on March 7 and returned on April 13, and in that interval of roughly forty days I visited numerous places in North, Central, and South America. In my capacity as the university's founder, I visited a number of universities and held discussions on such topics as the fundamental transformation required of contemporary civilization and the essential role of education. Relative to these issues, I made several proposals and also delivered lectures. I would like to begin today by sharing with you my impressions of the various places I visited.

I first visited the University of California, Berkeley, a renowned institution of higher learning with ten Nobel laureates on its faculty. At Berkeley, I enjoyed a dialogue with Chancellor Albert H. Bowker (1919–2008). Next, I went to the University of New Orleans where I talked with Chancellor Homer L. Hitt (1917–2008) on such subjects as my idea for a "United Nations for Education" and the creation of international assemblies as forerunners to such a body. These would include an international conference of university presidents, which would build ties among educational institutions, and a world federation of student councils, which would bring the students of various nations together. I am happy to say that Chancellor Hitt supported these ideas.

The subject of a United Nations for Education came up again later, during my talks with Vice Chancellor Norman P. Miller (1918–2004) of the University of California, Los Angeles. Vice Chancellor Miller and I thoroughly agreed on the importance of working for peace and the central role educational exchange can play in this. Also at UCLA, I delivered a lecture titled "The Enduring Self."

In addition to these universities in the United States, I visited the University of Panama and San Marcos University in Peru where I was able to engage in wide-ranging discussions. Rector Juan de Dios Guevara (1910–2000) of San Marcos University gave me a message for the students and faculty of Soka University which President Kazuo Takamatsu will convey to you in full.

Not long before I went to the Americas, I visited the Chinese University of Hong Kong and made similar proposals there, as I had already done last year at various universities in Europe. I am confident that our program to have more and more students and professors from other countries visit this university is now on a firm working basis, and I suspect the time will come when many of you also go abroad. As the university develops, there will be more and more to do. There will be many challenges, but I want you to know that in facing them is to be found purpose and satisfaction.

It is my firm resolve to take on any task to open new paths out into the world for you. Please know that wherever I travel around the world, and whomever I meet, you are always with me, in my heart, as my valued, trusted friends. I have, you might say, put down a few points in time and space. What I ask you now to do is join these points into lines and with these lines create the three-dimensional structure of world peace. This is the task that I am entrusting to you as my will and testament.

Today we have reached a point at which international political efforts to realize peace are at a deadlock. My proposal for a United Nations for Education is based on the belief that education represents humanity's final, and at the same time most certain, chance of achieving genuine world peace. It is for the purpose of setting the stage for a United Nations for Education that I advocate an international conference of university presidents, and it is to enable you and other students to actively take a stand for peace that I propose a world federation of student councils. These are all things that I cannot possibly bring into being on my own, so I want to ask you to work toward their realization.

More and more, the world will come to look upon Soka

University as a birthplace of new ideas, and it behooves you to develop into the kind of people—people of world stature and talent—who can meet the needs of that day. What I hope is that you will unite in your efforts to create a powerful movement for the promotion of mutual trust in the world through a vital program of international exchange among peoples.

When I went to San Marcos University, more than twenty professors sat in on my conference with the rector, and they each shared with me the maxim that guides their work. These, of course, are among the top-ranking educators in Peru and they all expressed interesting ideas, but I was particularly impressed by these words: "Professors and students alike must work with the masses. Together they must meet and overcome all difficulties until we reach the goal of wisdom and peace and happiness for humankind." The trouble with many contemporary intellectuals is that they habitually try to avoid such difficulties. This is something I am determined never to do. To justify its existence today, a university must strive with ordinary people to overcome difficulties and realize the most sublime objectives of humankind. My contention is that this always has been, and always will be, the mission of a university. I proclaim this again here with all my heart.

I am sure that if the teachers and students of Soka University and other universities throughout the world strive side by side with the people, we can arrive at the goal of peace for humankind. It is because of this belief that I have visited various universities and have made the proposals I mentioned. Now, more than anything else, I want you, who are the ones who will create the academic climate and tradition of this university, to take up this worthy cause.

A Student-Centered University

On the occasion of last year's entrance ceremony, I talked briefly about the origin and development of the university in history. At that time, I stressed that the university did not arise from structures or systems but from the determination and passion of young people seeking new knowledge and learning. There was, before anything, the aspiration of young people determined to absorb and make truth their own. These aspirations gave birth to teachers and instructors, and the human community of students and instructors working together in turn gave birth to the university. Fundamentally, then, the university began with thirst for knowledge and love of truth on the part of the students. This starting point is one to which the university must return, the impetus to which we must remain true. Without an active focus on the students, the university loses its purpose for being, its vital essence. Unfortunately, many Japanese universities today are suffering from stagnation and loss of direction, and the time has come when we must reawaken to the original purpose of university education.

What I want to ask of you who are entering Soka University today is that you regard yourselves no less than I as the founders and creators of this university. I hope you will never forget this point. And I urge you to be active participants in the work of building and protecting Soka University, not merely while you are students here, but throughout your lives.

When I was talking with the vice chancellor of San Marcos University about the gap between professors and students, he brought up two interesting points. First, he noted that dialogue between students and professors must continue without cease. Second, he said it must always be possible for students to play a responsible part in the university's affairs. I was struck by the fact that, in his earnest effort to grapple with the challenges facing his university, to find a way forward that suits the needs of the times, he has focused on giving students a leading and central role.

Here at Soka University, what I ask of you is not to wait passively for the university to do something for you but to engage—proudly, bravely, actively, passionately—in the construction work needed to make this university a new beacon of hope. There should indeed be a continuing dialogue, but do not forget that useful and profitable dialogue is based on responsibility and trust. It is not a matter of irresponsible, superficial disputation. Remember that this is your university, and that you are responsible for it. Remember that we are all united in making Soka University a driving force for the advancement of human culture. If you remember these things, your dialogues will be fruitful. We must create at this university a magnificent human community bound by a common sense of purpose and trust.

In this connection, I want to touch on the special nature and role of private universities, particularly in the case of Japan. Fundamentally, the significance of a private university is found in the autonomous pursuit of the ideals on which it was founded, unhampered by the intrusions of national authority. In such a university, it is possible to foster people of talent who have a genuinely global perspective and are engaged with the broad spectrum of issues affecting the future of humankind. It is the special function of a private university to send out into the world young people who can see beyond the narrow confines of state or nation, who possess the kind of encompassing vision that will enable them to make vital contributions on the world stage. In this way, the private university can support the work of transforming society in these deeply troubled times.

Like all universities, the private university must devote itself to scholarship and research, but in my opinion a private university should always have a liberal, lively atmosphere, completely free from the exclusive clannishness of academic factionalism. It is, I believe, the special mission of the private university to maintain crucial academic freedoms: the freedom to think, to pursue research and scholarly interests, and to give these expression. An institute of learning founded on a commitment to such principles will invariably yield independent and original research, fostering scholars rich in individuality and creativity. It is the duty of a private university to avoid being caught up in evanescent trends, and instead to sponsor long-range research of the widest possible scope.

The style of education and research that I have described as a positive potential of private universities is, I am convinced, the goal and mission that first motivated the emergence of the university within the vicissitudes of human history. Unfortunately, publicly funded, government-operated universities, for all their undeniably good features, can never fully ignore the demands and strictures placed on them by the state. The private university, while responding to the needs of one's own country and its people, is free to look beyond, to the needs of the world in general. In my opinion, the private university must be a stronghold that resists interference from government authorities and offers an unfailing haven for true learning and culture.

Ever since the Meiji era(1868–1912), it has been customary in Japan to regard the national or local government-funded universities as the main site for the education of youth and the promotion of culture. There has been a strong tendency, not only among educators but among people generally, to unquestioningly regard such public universities as the mainstream of education. As we consider the future of Japan and the rest of the world, however, it seems to me that if the spirit of the university is to be a living force in human society, we must reverse this situation and place private universities at the center and forefront of education.

What we need today is bright young people who have, through their experience of studying at a private university, acquired not only knowledge and wisdom but also the vigorous spirit of free and independent thought. When such young people travel the world, encountering and connecting with people across the globe, we will begin to see a new kind of fusion and exchange between cultures, individuals, and the peoples of various nations. We will, in short, have cultural interchange at the grassroots level, life-to-life exchanges among the ordinary citizens of the world, among all peoples, that bring forth the most positive aspects of each.

The day will come, I believe, when there will be cultural bridges linking the various peoples of the earth, when friendships will stretch across all national barriers, when people's hearts will respond joyfully to a peal announcing the birth of a new global culture, a new civilization for all humanity. And it is you who must become the envoys and the architects who create bridges of culture and peace linking the peoples of the world. It is you who must sound the great bell announcing to future generations the birth of a new global culture. Never forget that in the reverberations of that bell echo the yearnings of multitudes of people the world over.

Power and Wisdom

Recently, the French sociologist Georges Friedmann (1902–77), noted for his research on labor movements, published a book called *La Puissance et la sagesse* (The Power and Wisdom). Some of you may have read it in Japanese translation. The word *power* in the title refers to our power to control our environment by scientific or technological means. *Wisdom* means the intelligence to harness this power and use it creatively for the welfare of humanity. I won't attempt here to explain to you the contents of Friedmann's book, but I would like to make use of his distinction between power and wisdom.

From the start of the Meiji era until the end of World War II, Japanese education, and particularly college education, was all too narrowly aimed at the acquisition of power. The purpose was to absorb knowledge, master various technologies, and bring Japan up to the same level of power as the nations of Europe and America. This was the overriding goal to which Japanese education was consecrated. Underlying this idea was the fact that after long years of isolation, Japan was behind the Western nations in the field of science and technology, and there was a real danger that if Japan did not acquire power as quickly as possible, it might be colonized and trampled upon by these countries. And as it turned out, by virtue of the policy of pursuing national wealth and military prowess, Japan did manage to maintain its independence while the other countries of Asia were one by one deprived of theirs. Over time, however, continued pursuit of these policies—the worship of power and its aggressive use—culminated in defeat in war, an event of unprecedented enormity for Japan. This is a dearly paid-for historical lesson that you should engrave in your hearts.

Education that serves as a means to acquire power, that lacks the respect for human beings which is ultimately the lifeblood of education, that fails to inculcate in people a sense of the dignity of human life, can only produce people whose value lies in relation to the state or to corporations, people who are but cogs in the machinery of government or industry. It is crucial that you never forget that education has been put to such uses, that it has been made a means to such ends.

I do not deny that it is important to develop one's strengths and in this sense to acquire power, but this must always be accompanied by the development of wisdom. Wisdom, for its part, is rooted in human autonomy and agency, and begins from the Socratic injunction to self-knowledge. This is the foundation for awareness of the inviolable dignity and irreplaceable value of each human being. It is this awareness that can prevent people from being degraded into interchangeable "parts" in the mechanics of society.

In the final analysis, true learning and scholarship is found in knowledge of oneself. This is the ideal to which education and learning are directed at Soka University. There are many superlative universities and research institutions in the world where learning is directed to the acquisition of power. But what has the impact on humanity been? One might very well conclude that it has been the cruel emptiness and frustration of contemporary civilization.

I urge you to understand that your mission is to acquire the wisdom that will enable you to use all forms of power for the sake of the happiness and peace of humankind. Know yourselves, and armed with that knowledge, study. I want you to think of all things in relation to yourselves as human beings, to reexamine the meaning of knowledge, technology, and art to humanity. For only this can revive and restore humankind. I pray for your personal growth and development, for I am certain that the accumulated impact of such small and painstaking efforts will be a great renaissance of human culture.

The renowned French art historian René Huyghe (1906–97) recently gave a lecture at the University of Tokyo titled

"*Formes et forces*" (Forms and Forces in Nature and Art). If I may paraphrase his comments, I believe his main point was this: the crisis of our times is a crisis of civilization, the danger of materialism carried too far. The failing of our culture is that everything becomes compartmentalized and we lose sight of the whole. Human civilization is a single indivisible entity, and intellectuals should use all of their knowledge and power on behalf of civilization. The crisis we face today is not merely a social or political crisis but a fundamental crisis of civilization. I am, by the way, scheduled to meet with M. Huyghe tomorrow evening.

Open the Door of Your Life

You are all destined to achieve great things in the world of the twenty-first century, and here I would like to speak to you for a few moments simply as a friend.

Last year, when I spoke to the members of the entering class, I asked them to strive to be creative individuals. Following up on that, today I would like to discuss what I refer to as "creative life"—the creative impulse and capacities that are inherent in life itself. I don't intend to enter into a difficult philosophical disquisition or try to offer universally applicable definitions. Rather, very simply, I would urge you, as you travel along the long and precious road of life, never to become gloomy travelers who are shadowed by a sense of failure or defeat. To this end, and in the hope your futures will be filled with honor and glory, I would like to share with you something from my own experience.

The times when I have most intensely felt and experienced the inner reality of creation have been those times when I have thrown myself wholeheartedly into a task, when I have carried through with that task to the very end. At such times, I experience a dramatically expanded sense of self. I can almost hear the joyous yell of victory issuing from the depths of my being. This sense of fulfillment and joy is the crystallization of all the effort—each drop of sweat, each tear—expended to reach that moment. Life's inherent creativity, its dynamic vitality, is brought to the surface only through the strenuous exertions of a life of consistent action. Such a way of life will meet with storms and heavy rains, times of seeming defeat. But the creative essence of life is never crushed or vanquished by such things. It is sustained by knowledge of the brilliant rainbow whose bright arch will eventually stretch across the inner expanse of your being.

Indulgence and indolence produce nothing creative. Complaints and evasions reflect a cowardly spirit; they corrupt and undermine life's natural creative thrust. When life is denuded of the will to struggle creatively, it sinks into a state of hellish destructiveness directed at all that lives. Never for an instant forget the effort to renew your life, to build yourself anew. Creativity means to push open the heavy, groaning doorway of life itself. This is not an easy task. Indeed, it may be the most severely challenging struggle there is. For opening the door to your own life is in the end more difficult than opening the door to all the mysteries of the universe. But to do so is to vindicate your existence as human beings. Even more, it is the mode of existence that is authentically attuned to the innermost truths of life itself; it makes us worthy of the gift of life.

There is no way of life more desolate or more pitiful than one of ignorance of the fundamental joy that issues from the struggle to generate and regenerate one's own life from within. To be human is much more than the mere biological facts of standing erect and exercising reason and intelligence.

The full and genuine meaning of our humanity is found in tapping the creative fonts of life itself. The struggle to create new life from within is a truly wonderful thing. There is found the brilliant wisdom that guides and directs the workings of reason; the light of insight that penetrates the farthest reaches of the universe; the undaunted will to see justice done that meets and challenges all the assaults of evil; the spirit of unbounded care that embraces all who suffer. When these are fused with that energy of compassion that pours forth from the deepest sources of cosmic life, an ecstatic rhythm arises to color the lives of all people.

As you meet various trials and difficulties, thus polishing all the many facets of the jewel that is life, you will learn to walk that supreme pathway of humanity. Of this, I am confident; and I am confident too that those who embrace life's native creativity now stand and will continue to stand in the vanguard of history. Bringing the creativity of life to its fullest flowering is the work of human revolution. Carrying out this kind of human revolution is your mission now as it will be throughout your lives.

The nineteenth-century French poet and writer Charles Péguy (1873–1914) said, "The crisis of education is not a crisis of education, but a crisis of life."[1] The crisis we face today strikes at the very roots of education and learning. And yet it is in education and learning that we will find the doorway to the future. And that is why I put so much faith in Soka University.

My friends, may this day be the beginning of four happy, meaningful years for you. To the professors of Soka University as well as to the administrators and current students: I ask you to take good care of this year's new students, for they are the future's treasure.

Youthful Efforts Become
a Lifetime Treasure

At Soka Women's College, Tokyo, October 1, 2002.

FIRST OF ALL, as the founder of Soka Women's College, I would like to thank you for choosing to attend this school. Please convey my very best regards to your parents.

All of the efforts you make will become a treasure in your life—a treasure that will last a lifetime, a treasure of happiness.

Those who spend their youth in frivolous, shallow pursuits, simply content to have a good time and enjoy themselves, invariably regret their folly later on. They ultimately end up suffering. Life isn't always a bed of roses.

It is in scaling life's mountains, crossing life's valleys, and traversing life's precipitous peaks, ever advancing with integrity and fortitude, that happiness is found. A magnificent palace can be built only when we work unceasingly on its construction day after day with all our might, until it is finally completed. The same is true of life.

We study in order to become happy. The purpose of both life and learning is to become happy. If we are ignorant, we will be looked down on—in society, in married life, by those around us, and perhaps even by our own children. That is a sad thing, indeed.

Out in society, there are many different kinds of people: malicious people who seek to undermine and deceive others;

arrogant people who scorn and despise others. We study so that we can prevail over such people, succeed in all our endeavors, and lead fulfilling lives.

Knowledge alone cannot guarantee happiness. We need to have wisdom if we are to live wisely. Knowledge is like a pump that draws up the water of wisdom. Cultivating wisdom is a shortcut to happiness.

I hope that all of you will strive to become people who possess rich wisdom and common sense. Please develop the kind of character that others look up to and admire. I would like you to work harmoniously with others, to lead others, and to live in a way that is respected by all. Each day you study at this school is immensely important toward that end.

My young friends, please make good books your close companions. Reading good books—mind-enriching novels, the great classics, and world literature—will become a treasure of your youth.

Many intelligent and informed people decry the growing prevalence of sleazy tabloid journalism we see today. "Journalists responsible for such scurrilous and defamatory reporting," they observe, "sow only trouble in society. While gloating over others' misfortune, they are oblivious to the fact that they themselves are steering a direct course to misery."

I hope you will always walk the path leading to happiness.

Allow me to talk a little about a novel by the French writer Guy de Maupassant (1850–93) titled *A Life*. The story opens with the protagonist, Jeanne, as a young woman in her late teens.

The daughter of country nobility, Jeanne has grown up sheltered from life's harsh realities. She glows with a sweet, unsullied loveliness. She also lives in a beautiful chateau. Brimming with hope and deeply romantic, she dreams of the future. Just imagining her yet-unknown lover fills her heart with joy.

Eventually, she meets the son of another aristocratic family, and they marry in a lavish ceremony attended by many well-wishers. Jeanne looks set to enjoy every happiness in life. But once she is married, she finds that she and her husband have nothing in common. He is a source of continual disappointment and disillusionment.

Her husband betrays her, her beloved mother dies, and then her husband dies too. Seeking to erase these distressing memories from her mind, Jeanne throws herself into raising her son, who becomes her one happiness in life. But this, too, turns out badly, as her son, spoiled by her indulgence, becomes a wild and degenerate young man. He ceaselessly badgers his mother for money and squanders the family fortune.

Eventually, the now elderly Jeanne must give up her beloved chateau; she is consumed by a deep spiritual loneliness. Entrusted with the care of her granddaughter, her sole remaining joy in life is lavishing her affection on the little girl.

This novel was written more than a century ago (in 1883), and both society and values have changed since then, but the questions it raises—What is life? What is happiness? What fulfills the human spirit?—transcend time and are equally relevant today.

The Vital Importance of Human Revolution

Life is harsh, complicated, and often baffling. Many people may feel that though they strive and strive, all their efforts are in vain, and that though they seek happiness, all they encounter is a string of misfortune.

You are young. Right now you think you'll never grow old. However, no one can escape the universal human sufferings of birth, old age, sickness, and death. This, too, is a harsh reality.

There are people who betray others. There are cowards who abandon their beliefs in a crisis.

There are people who spend their whole lives lamenting their bad luck and the cruel hand that fate has dealt them. I absolutely never want any of you to live your lives this way.

Where, then, can we find the key for turning our lives in a positive direction? Absolutely vital in this question is the philosophy of human revolution. Human revolution offers the only certain path to happiness and victory in life. Human revolution means transforming our lives from unhappiness to happiness.

The challenge is transforming our lives so that we are no longer swept along by force of habit or at the mercy of the whims of destiny. The incredible power to do that already exists inside you.

Forge a solid self, and develop within you the power to attract happiness to your life. Then you yourself will be happy and fulfilled, and you will be able to lead your family, your relatives, and your friends to happiness too.

We only live this precious life but once. Please make continual efforts, steadily overcoming life's challenges one step at a time, until you ultimately achieve a life in which all of your wishes are realized. May all of you, without exception, become happy. That is my sincerest wish. That is the purpose of your two years at Soka Women's College.

Among your predecessors at this school are many highly accomplished women. I frequently receive tidings of their activities and of the trust and recognition they have won in society. This brings me great joy.

I hope that all of you will take immense pride in studying at this unsurpassed institution of higher learning and make your time here the most wonderful and satisfying days of your youth.

Caught Napping in Class

I also receive various reports on the activities of our precious Soka University and Soka Women's College students every day.

For instance, I heard that in one recent class, some students were caught napping, but the instructor didn't say anything and just continued patiently with his lecture. Later, out of concern for the students, he called them to his office and asked them why they were napping in class.

The first student answered honestly that he had been working at his part-time job until late the night before and he just fell asleep. No doubt he *was* tired; to him the instructor's brilliant lecture probably sounded like a gentle lullaby!

A second student said that he wasn't sleeping at all, but that he was better able to absorb the lecture's content if he listened with his eyes shut. Obviously, he has a way with words!

A third student said that he always got sleepy when he studied. He apologized for behaving inconsiderately to his teacher and his fellow students and he said he knew that he would have a terrible time when exams rolled around. He then said, with deep self-reflection: "This is the last time I will fall asleep in class. I am determined to carry out my human revolution. If I ever want to make something of myself, I have to get serious about my studies. I now realize how important this is."

As the other students there listened to his vow, they realized how their teacher must feel when, doing his best to give a good lecture, he saw students sleeping in class. When they looked at the situation from their teacher's viewpoint, they felt so bad that they, too, renewed their determination never to sleep in class again.

Of course, students shouldn't sleep during class, but when I heard about this episode, I was impressed with these students. I think the reason that the instructor didn't say anything during class but just let them sleep was the great trust he had in his students. I was pleased by the students' straightforwardness, which is why I shared this story with you.

Seek Out Difficult Challenges!

Madame Deng Yingchao (1904–92) is revered in China as the "mother of the people." In the midst of the Sino-Japanese War of 1937–45, she called out to young Chinese women students: "You are the bell that announces the dawn. You are the sun of the new day."[1] How this clarion call must have encouraged them!

Our voices are important. In particular, the voices of women have the power to make people feel more energetic, optimistic, and full of life.

From her teens, Madame Deng courageously leaped into the tempest of the revolution. She was surrounded by enemies front and behind; she never knew when she might be arrested or killed. That was how she spent her youth.

My message to you, therefore, is: Please don't spend your youth avoiding hardship and taking the path of least resistance. Please seek out difficult challenges and work hard. And if you are going to take on hardships, let it be for the sake of a high ideal. Don't stay closed up in your own tiny shell, pursue your studies with the high ideals of helping your friends and contributing to society and humanity. This is where the true significance of the pursuit of learning lies.

In addition, the greater your goals, the greater growth you can achieve. Also, when you have a great objective, you'll be able to bravely endure and overcome any obstacles or difficulties you may encounter.

Madame Deng also told the women students, "Your suffering sisters are fervently awaiting the illumination you will bring them!"[2]

With the same urgency, I wish to say to you, the students of Soka Women's College, "Your sisters in the twenty-first century who will follow after you are awaiting your growth and development!"

Please start from what you can challenge right now, striving to broaden your own knowledge and to expand your circle of friends—both of which are a precious treasure—as you advance together toward peace and happiness.

My wife and I enjoyed an unchanging friendship with Madame Deng for as long as she lived. We met a total of eight times, in China and Japan. She trusted us from the bottom of her heart, and twice she invited us to her Beijing home, which held many memories of her husband, Premier Zhou Enlai (1898–1976). On one occasion, gazing at the two of us intently, she said, "You remind me of my husband and me when we were young." This remains one of my fondest memories.

Six Guidelines for Women Leaders

Madame Deng offered young women six guidelines for being a good leader.

The first is "Protect the ideals of the revolution." Ideals are essential in youth and in life. A person without ideals is sad; whereas those who have ideals that they pursue throughout life will remain young at heart, no matter what their age.

The second guideline is "Be courageous." The basis for victory in life is courage, is bravery. In particular, I would like women to be even more courageous than men. When women are courageous, peace in both the family and society is protected.

There are many women leaders in the world, including presidents of nations and presidents of institutions of higher education. I have also spoken with many women leaders, and all of them carved out their path in life through the power of courage.

Madame Deng's third guideline is "Never forget to be responsible and earnest." A person who has a sense of responsibility is earnest, and an earnest person is strong. Earnestness is a wonderful quality.

For example, all of you study late into the night. You are advancing in the right direction. How happy this must make your parents. Their joy probably cannot be expressed in words. You are perhaps still too young to be able to appreciate how they feel.

In any event, please never forget to be responsible and earnest.

The fourth guideline Madame Deng offered is "Cultivate patience and perseverance." Study requires patience. Sport requires patience. Even helping with household chores requires patience! Only the things you obtain through patience and perseverance will shine as your eternal and indestructible treasures.

The fifth guideline is "Be sincere and humble." Sincerity

isn't simply a passive attitude. For you as students, being sincere means studying diligently. This is responding sincerely to your teachers and to your parents, who are supporting you. And humility isn't hesitation or shrinking back. It is living your life earnestly and honestly—in school as a student; in your family, as a daughter; and if you marry, as a wife.

Humility means doing your very best in your present circumstances and situation, working together harmoniously with those around you. Arrogance, on the other hand, is doing whatever you please, without thinking about anyone else. Arrogance is wrong and will bring one misfortune. Humility is right and will lead one to happiness.

Madame Deng's sixth guideline is "Continue to study unceasingly," for the sake of your personal happiness and to win a splendid life. We must continue to learn and study throughout life. Faith is the ultimate expression of that process. I hope that all of you will continue to study and learn as long as you live.

These are the six guidelines that Madame Deng entrusted to women of a new age.[3]

"Holding Aloft the Torch of Practice"

In closing, I would like to share with you a poem that Madame Deng wrote at the age of nineteen. The title is "The Torch of Practice."

> Holding aloft the torch of practice,
> Illuminating the way ahead of us,
> We advance step after step.
>
> . . . .

> We who hold aloft the torch of practice
> Will dye the road before us,
> One drop after another,
> With our hot crimson blood.[4]

Life is making practical efforts. It is challenging ourselves. It is advancing.

Your youth never comes again. Please leave behind some achievement, please create something as a record of your existence in this world.

In praise of your daily struggles, let me say, "Bravo to the students of Soka Women's College!" Thank you so much for the opportunity to speak to you today.

I pray for your health and growth. Please give my regards to your parents. Take care!

The University of the Twenty-First Century—Cradle of Global Citizens

Message to the first commencement ceremony of Soka University of America, Aliso Viejo, May 22, 2005.

T O THE FIRST graduating class of Soka University of America (SUA), Aliso Viejo, who are my life, my hope, my pride, I wish to extend my heartfelt congratulations on the marvelous occasion of your graduation.

Each of you is a great pioneer, an honored founder of SUA. All of you are victors. Each of you is a brilliant, precious jewel; you possess a noble mission.

While you could have attended some other prestigious university with time-honored traditions, you chose instead to study at this newborn institution, Soka University of America. Gathering here, you have worked with the subsequent entering classes to successfully establish the solid foundations for the future development of SUA.

I wish I could fly to the campus that stands on the hills of Aliso Viejo, shake hands with each of you, thank you, and congratulate you on your successful graduation and on the indomitable spirit with which you have earned this victory. Such are the sentiments that fill my heart now.

It is my determination to continue to watch over you, to pray for your health and growth, that your lives may be crowned with glory and triumph. This I will do throughout my life—for all eternity. My heart is always with you.

With my heart full of deep feelings of gratitude, I wish to offer some words and thoughts to celebrate your new departure.

The Source of Strength

When I think of you earnestly pursuing your studies far from home, I am reminded of Dr. Wangari Maathai (1940–2011) of Kenya, whom I met in Tokyo this past February and who also devoted her youth to study and learning. As you know, she is an environmental activist and a recipient of last year's Nobel Peace Prize.

For some thirty years, Dr. Maathai has struggled against and overcome harassment, persecution, and oppression as she has courageously led a grassroots movement of women to plant trees in order to enhance the lives of the Kenyan people and protect the environment.

Her persistence has produced results. The reforestation work that started from seven saplings has now seen more than thirty million trees planted throughout Kenya and Africa, supporting the lives of countless people and contributing to the peace and security of the region.

Dr. Maathai is a woman of brilliant intellect with a warm and embracing character. She possesses a robust spirit that remains unbent before all oppression. Where did she develop and forge these qualities and strengths? She has cited the important influence of her experience of studying in the United States, where she was blessed with good friends and mentors.

She has written that the professors at the college where

she studied cared for her as if she were their daughter. One professor whom she respected deliberately placed her office in a location where the students would pass by frequently. The door was always open, and the professor smiled gently on each of the students as they passed.

Dr. Maathai describes this experience and her profound gratitude to her teachers: "They did everything to help me, educate me, and enrich my life. I had already benefited from a full scholarship, yet I continued to receive so much more."[1]

After completing a master's course at graduate school in the US, she returned to Kenya, receiving her doctorate from the University of Nairobi and becoming the first woman to earn a doctoral degree at a Kenyan university. Thus she began her struggle for the happiness of her country and its people.

Since her student days, Dr. Maathai's deep resolve had been to return to Africa and work for the people. A professor who taught Dr. Maathai in her youth stated with deep emotion, "We get many students who say that, then become successful and decide to stay in this country [America], but she kept her word."[2]

I hope that all of today's graduates will likewise treasure, throughout your lives, the resolves you have made here at SUA, the vows you have shared here with your friends. A truly outstanding person is, I believe, one who never forgets the vows of youth and lives a life dedicated to contributing to the well-being of others.

At the same time, please remember that it is because of your parents and family, who have offered their support despite all difficulties, that we are able to celebrate today's joyous occasion. I hope that you will be the kind of people who remember and deeply appreciate this debt of gratitude.

Further, I wish to express my most sincere thanks to all the members of the faculty and administration who have worked so hard to create a new path where none existed before.

Finally, I wish to also extend my appreciation to all our neighbors and friends who have supported SUA over the years, and to all those people in the United States and throughout the world who have been earnestly yearning for and assisting the development of this new university.

For the graduates, today marks the start of a new phase as you step out on the main stage of your lives. I can fully sense the excitement with which your hearts must be filled, the feeling of great dreams taking flight into the future.

It is my fervent wish that each of you will blaze your own path of mission as a founder, pioneer, and eternal comrade of Soka University of America. Please create the kind of life, leave behind you the kind of personal history, so that you can proudly say, "Here stands a member of the first graduating class of SUA!"

The Challenge of the University

Today I would like to offer some thoughts on the role of the university in the twenty-first century, so we can think together about the role and mission that SUA must fulfill.

In April last year, I met with Dr. M. S. Swaminathan (1925–), president of the Pugwash Conferences on Science and World Affairs, an organization of scientists working toward disarmament and the renunciation of war. Dr. Swaminathan is an internationally renowned agricultural scientist famous for his vital contributions to resolving India's food crisis.

During a meeting in which we exchanged views on various global issues, I was particularly struck by this statement by Dr. Swaminathan. He first stressed humanity's crucial need for a revolution in educational practices. He then noted that there is a pronounced tendency for people to assert their rights without a corresponding willingness to accept responsibility. He urged the importance of spiritual discipline and said that we must each bear a strong sense of responsibility, not as a master of the earth but as one of the earth's constituent members. This is an extremely important point indeed.

When we look at our world today, regional conflicts and ethnic strife are growing ever more intense, and the chain reactions of violence and hatred appear to continue without any end in sight. Global challenges such as those of the environment, food production, and energy supply have grown more acute, bringing humanity face to face with an unprecedented crisis.

But we must remember that all these crises are human in their origin; it is we humans ourselves who have brought them on. It thus stands to reason that if we can succeed in bringing together the wisdom of humanity, we will be able without fail to meet these challenges and find a path to their resolution. We not only can but must find the means to effect the transformation of the age in which we live. To this end, the inner reform and spiritual growth of individual human beings is absolutely essential.

In particular, what is needed now are global citizens who take a truly planetary perspective and are committed to the well-being of humankind as a whole. It is imperative to foster such individuals and to generate wide-reaching solidarity among them. Education must be reformed and revolutionized to respond to this need. In this regard, the mission and responsibility of the university, as the highest seat of learning, are crucially important.

What kind of university can stand at the forefront of the

process of revolutionizing education in the twenty-first century? In order to explore this vast and daunting question, I would first like to trace in overview the history of the development of the modern university.

Birth of the Modern University

It is said that the Western university finds its origin in medieval Italy at the University of Bologna. In June 1994, I was invited and had the opportunity to present a lecture there.

Known as the *mater nobilium studiorum,* the "mother of noble studies," the University of Bologna developed through the passionate yearning of students to learn and the earnest determination of teachers to fulfill that desire. Rooted in the traditions of the medieval university, the University of Berlin (Berliner Universität), established in 1810, marks the start of the history of the modern university.

At the University of Berlin, a method of instruction centered on joint research by students and professors was adopted. At the time, it was common for students simply to listen passively to the professor's lectures. Scholarship was typically understood as the process of absorbing established forms of knowledge, and there was little room for students to raise a critical view. Professors could neglect their own research efforts without exposing themselves to criticism. There are those who describe the decades leading up to the establishment of the University of Berlin as an era of stagnation.

Based on the vision of Johann Gottlieb Fichte (1762–1814) and the von Humboldt brothers, the founding of the University of Berlin was a breakthrough moment in the history of the university. At the heart of this was the principle of education through research, in which students are accorded equal standing to professors in the quest for knowledge and truth. The seminar system, where students present their research findings and all participants engage in discussion and debate, is said to have started at the University of Berlin and other German universities.

The elder of the von Humboldt brothers, Wilhelm (1767–1835), figured importantly in the general plan of educational reform in Prussia at the time. He describes the motivating spirit behind his efforts in this way:

> The university teacher is therefore no longer a teacher and the student no longer someone merely engaged in the learning process but a person who undertakes his own research, while the professor directs his research and supports him in it.[3]

Teachers and students mutually inspiring and stimulating one another in a vibrant process of learning through unfettered dialogue and debate, together scaling the summits of knowledge—herein lies an ideal vision of university education.

The introduction of the teaching principles of the University of Berlin marked the start of a period of dramatic development for German universities. A century later, by the early years of the twentieth century, German universities were leading the world in the number of Nobel Prize recipients for the natural sciences.

At the same time, we must be aware of the pitfalls of education that has developed an excessive focus on specialized knowledge. The Spanish philosopher José Ortega y Gasset (1883–1955), for example, offers this bleak vision in *Mission of the University*, published in 1930: "the astounding spectacle of how brutal, how stupid, and yet how aggressive is the man learned in one thing and fundamentally ignorant of all else."[4]

For Ortega y Gasset, the core mission of university education is the transmission and fostering of culture, which he termed "the *vital* system of ideas of a period"[5]—the kind of philosophy or spiritual compass that can guide people along the correct path of life in complex and confusing times. For him, culture is "precisely the opposite of external ornament."[6] Rather, it is what "saves human life from being a mere disaster; it is what enables man to live a life which is something above meaningless tragedy or inward disgrace."[7]

Some time back, I had the privilege of visiting the Simon Wiesenthal Center Museum of Tolerance in Los Angeles. There I saw a reproduction of the site of the Wannsee Conference, the meeting of high-level Nazi officials where the extermination of Europe's Jews was planned. It is said that of the fourteen participants in this meeting, eight were holders of doctoral degrees.

Similarly, it was members of Japan's intellectual elite, trained at the nation's leading academic institutions, who supported and propelled the madness of Japanese militarism.

These are stark lessons from history demonstrating the depths of cruelty and barbarism to which intellectuals who lack a guiding philosophy can sink. People whose character has not been refined by genuine culture are capable of brutal acts that negate and deny all humanity.

In contrast to Ortega y Gasset's emphasis on the importance of culture and student-centered education, the German philosopher Karl Jaspers (1883–1969) called for the cultivation of human personality and character through research. In May of 1945, immediately after the fall of Nazi Germany, he wrote *Die idee der universitat* (*The Idea of the University),* in which he called for a reconstruction of the universities that had been ravaged by the Nazis. He himself had endured persecution at their hands.

Jaspers states, "Because truth is accessible to systematic search, research is the foremost concern of the university."[8] And, "Only he who himself does research can really teach."[9]

For Jaspers, research constitutes the very essence of the university. To what goal or end is this research to be directed? For Jaspers this is, very simply, humanity. As he states: "Seeking truth and the improvement of mankind, the university aims to stand for man's humanity *par excellence. Humanitas* is part of its very fiber, no matter how often and how deeply that term has changed its meaning."[10]

Jaspers believed that "ideally the relation between professor and student involves a Socratic equality of status with a mutual stress on standard, not on authority."[11] He emphasized that individuals whose intellect and character have been cultivated through dialogue and pursuit of truth based on this kind of mentor-student relationship are those most capable of contributing to society.

A Philosophy of Global Citizenship

The approaches taken by Ortega y Gasset and Jaspers may differ, but both concur that culture and humanity must be the core goals to which university education aspires. In both, we note a shared concern that without the kind of philosophy that will direct it to the goal of human happiness, the most advanced knowledge will not only be useless, it will be dangerous.

The darkness enveloping this chaotic age is deep. In such an era, nothing is more sought or required than the brilliant light of culture that shines only from those who have polished their wisdom and character.

Culture may be thought of as the wisdom that enables us to make the best use of knowledge. The American philosopher John Dewey (1859–1952) consistently stressed the importance of wisdom above mere knowledge. In the same way, my own mentor and second president of the Soka Gakkai, Josei Toda (1900–58), considered the confusion of wisdom and knowledge the crucial misapprehension of contemporary civilization. The relationship between knowledge and wisdom may be likened to that of a pump and the pure, refreshing water it brings to the surface. Knowledge is actually the means by which wisdom is brought forth and manifested from within.

Knowledge alone cannot give rise to value. It is only when knowledge is guided by wisdom that value—defined by the father of *soka*, or value-creating, education, Tsunesaburo Makiguchi (1871–1944), as beauty, gain, and good—is created. The font of wisdom is found in the following elements: an overarching sense of purpose, a powerful sense of responsibility, and finally, the compassionate desire to contribute to the welfare of humankind. When wisdom arises from such wellsprings, it nourishes the kind of inner strength that remains unmoved by the superficial judgments of society and can acutely discern what is of genuine value and what is, in fact, detrimental.

Soka University of America was founded as a liberal arts college in the hope and desire that all who learn here will be able to develop and polish the inner strength needed to generate limitless value from all forms of knowledge, to forge, in your capacity as global citizens, the peace and happiness of humankind.

Here I would like to consider some ideas about the kind of

philosophy that can guide this process of value creation for the benefit of humankind.

Respect for Life

The first thing I would stress is that this must be a philosophy of absolute respect and reverence for life.

I am currently conducting a dialogue with Dr. Joseph Rotblat (1908–2005), the renowned physicist and champion of peace who for many years has dedicated himself to the abolition of nuclear weapons. I am certain that the encouragement Dr. Rotblat shared with you here at SUA in the immediate aftermath of the September 11, 2001, terror attacks remains deeply engraved in your hearts. Dr. Rotblat has offered his heartfelt felicitations to all the graduates.

The focus of my ongoing dialogue with Dr. Rotblat is precisely the philosophy of reverence for life.

During World War II, feeling the need to respond to the threat that the Nazis would develop nuclear weapons, Dr. Rotblat participated in the Manhattan Project, the Allied nuclear weapons development effort. However, when he saw that Germany had given up on its efforts to develop such weapons and sensing that the true purpose of the project was the postwar containment of the Soviet Union, he courageously resigned from the project, the only scientist to do so before the completion of its purpose. He experienced immense hardship as he was treated as a communist spy and made the target of all manner of groundless slander.

Despite these difficulties, he continued to act in accord with his inner convictions. What was it that enabled him to do this? He cites the horrific experience of World War I, which left his consciousness indelibly marked with the awareness that war is an absolute evil. As a result of that war, his family lost all their possessions, making his childhood years a continuous struggle against illness and hunger.

Spurred by this experience, the youthful Dr. Rotblat made the determination to use the power of science to create a world in which there would be no need for war. He committed himself to the work of eliminating the causes of people's suffering and contributing to their happiness. This was the determination made in his youth. Later, when the Nazis invaded Poland, Dr. Rotblat lost his beloved wife in the Holocaust.

This year he turns ninety-seven; having surmounted all manner of obstacles, he continues to this day to work for the cause of peace and the sanctity of life.

Unless acted on, even the ideal of reverence for life can end up being a mere slogan without the power to transform reality. It must, therefore, be established as a genuine philosophy in our own hearts and in the hearts of others. We must put this philosophy into practice through concrete actions for peace, working one step at a time toward its realization.

In the statement he made in 1957 calling for the prohibition of nuclear weapons, Josei Toda denounced their use as a "demonic, satanic, and monstrous" threat to human existence and declared his determination to expose and "declaw" the monstrous nature lurking behind such weapons. This was his lion's roar.

With this, he declared his determination to challenge and combat all forms of evil and violence, ignorance and prejudice. To achieve this, he consistently urged people to commit themselves to the cause of "human revolution"—a struggle to realize a fundamental, positive transformation in the depths of our own and others' lives.

The focus of *soka*, or value-creating, education must always be the achievement of this kind of human revolution.

Respect for Cultural Difference

The next point I would like to stress is respect for cultural difference, developing the capacity to respect cultures that are different from our own.

Human history has seen all too many clashes and conflicts rooted in prejudice against and misunderstanding of other cultures, with people incited to hatred and hostility. Indeed, this is the tragic destiny we must transform.

The Mohandas (1869–1948) and Kasturba Gandhi (1869–1944) Hall on the SUA campus bears the name of a great leader of nonviolent struggle. In the past, I had several unforgettable opportunities to meet and talk with Dr. B. N. Pande (1906–98), member of Rajya Sabha (the Council of States) and vice chairman of Gandhi Smriti and Darshan Samiti (the Gandhi Memorial Hall). The late Dr. Pande took part in the struggle for Indian independence as one of Mahatma Gandhi's closest disciples; during one of our meetings, he proudly shared with me the following episode, which he cited as an example of how deeply Gandhi's philosophy has influenced India's young people.

The incident occurred when a mob of fanatical Hindus attacked a student hostel where both Hindu and Muslim students were living, all working to complete their academic theses. The rabble called on the Hindu students living in the hostel to come out, saying they would be safe. The Muslim students were to remain inside. If no one came out, the mob would set fire to the building with everyone in it.

The students all refused to come out, saying that unless everyone's safety was assured, they would all stay inside; the mob could set fire to the building if they wanted to. Eventually, the army arrived and the students were able to evacuate the building.

At this time, the mob threatened that only the Hindu students could bring out their books and papers. But again, the Hindu students refused to accept special treatment from the mob—if you intend to burn the theses of the Muslim students, burn ours too! In the end, the building was burned and, with it, all the students' papers.

Dr. Pande spoke with one of the Hindu students, who had spent three years writing his doctoral thesis. When he asked the student if he wasn't bitter, the student responded: "What could I be bitter about? My conscience is perfectly clear. I acted in accordance with Gandhiji's teachings. That is our spirit." He had protected, to the very end, his fellow students whose religion was different from his own.

Students from more than thirty countries are studying at SUA. Truly, you are the world in miniature. With mutual respect for differences in values and cultures, you have learned from one another, forging treasured friendships. I imagine there were many times when you found the differences in cultures and ways of thinking confusing, even bewildering. But I am certain that these experiences will all be an inestimable treasure and asset for you in your role as future leaders.

However the times and the world may change, I hope the graduates of SUA will always treasure, throughout your lives, the precious bonds of friendship that you have developed studying together here on this hilltop campus in Aliso Viejo. Please continue to build and spread a global network of friendship that unites the hearts of the world's people in trust and mutual understanding.

You are the eternal members of the first graduating class of SUA. As global citizens who have learned and absorbed Soka humanism, I know you are dedicated to living always at the forefront of efforts to realize a human future of creative coexistence.

Remembering the People

The third point I wish to stress is the spirit of working for the common people, sharing their joys and sorrows. This determination and conviction is the essential foundation for global citizenship. The university must be a place that fosters people of talent committed to serving the needs of all those who, much as they might have wished, have not been able to receive higher education. This has been my consistent assertion over the years.

Moscow State University recently celebrated the 250th anniversary of its founding. The rector of the university, Dr. Victor A. Sadovnichy (1939–), has shared with me the following episode from his own life.

When he was young, his circumstances made it appear impossible that he would ever be able to go to university. He left his native village and engaged in hard labor in a coal mine while continuing to study.

Initially, he applied for admittance to an agricultural college. But when his team leader at the coal mine heard this, he urged the young Dr. Sadovnichy to apply to Moscow State University, assuring him there was still time. This man even went to the post office and got the original application back, resending it to Moscow State University.

Without such heartfelt support and encouragement, Dr. Sadovnichy stated, he would never have studied at, much less become rector of, Moscow State University. Dr. Sadovnichy told me that the determination to do something for the people who believed in him and sought his growth is at the heart of his own efforts to assure that Moscow State University continues to develop as an institution dedicated to the welfare of ordinary citizens.

Soka University of America is a university of, by, and for the common people. It embodies the intense desire and expectation on the part of the world's ordinary citizens that you will grow into people capable of contributing to the realization of peace. In places and countries throughout the world, there are people who want you to have the kind of education they themselves were not able to enjoy. Concurring with the founding ideals of SUA, they have offered their generous support. These are people who, far from affluent themselves, have made sincere donations to the university in the hope that they will be of help to those who study here.

I ask that you never forget the noble, precious hearts of your fellow citizens. I ask that you live the kind of lives that will be a sincere requital of this debt of gratitude. And I ask that each one of you become the kind of strong and capable person who continues always to proudly tread the path of contribution to society, working for the happiness of the world's ordinary citizens. For it is precisely in such a life that you will find your highest pride, purpose, and joy.

Achieving Democracy

The fourth point I wish to stress is that education and learning are, more than anything else, the motive forces propelling the development of democracy. John Dewey and other American philosophers have offered us some of the most profound insights into this reality.

As Dewey repeatedly emphasized: "A democracy is more than a form of government."[12] For Dewey, universal suffrage, majority rule, and other forms of political organization are best understood as means for the realization of genuine democracy. He went so far as to state: "It is a form of idolatry to erect means into the end which they serve."[13]

The great poet Walt Whitman (1819–92) declared, "Democracy too is law, and of the strictest, amplest kind."[14] And, "Law is the unshakable order of the universe forever."[15]

Democracy is a way of life whose purpose is to enable people to achieve spiritual autonomy, live in mutual respect, and enjoy happiness. It can also be understood as an expression of human wisdom deployed toward the goal of creative coexistence. It is in this sense that it can be understood as a universal principle.

But here we must bear in mind Dewey's stern warning. People tend to think of democracy as something that is fixed and complete, which can simply be passed from the hands of one generation to the next. But this is not the case: "Every generation has to accomplish democracy over again for itself."[16]

The continuous effort to accomplish democracy was identified by Dewey as "the greatest experiment of humanity."[17] The work of pursuing and carrying out this noble experiment is the daily task of education. This is because a genuinely democratic society cannot be realized by authority or force applied from without. The proper path involves drawing forth and unleashing the capacities inherent in people, which are then directed with autonomy and spontaneity toward the construction of a democratic society. Dewey's insight was that education holds the key to making this possible.

I wish therefore to deeply affirm once more that the primal mission of the university is to temper and forge democratic ideals, rooting them in society as a form of service to all of humankind.

The Spirit of Mentor and Disciple

In the words of Leo Tolstoy (1828–1910): "Religious teaching, that is, the explanation of the purpose and meaning of life, should be the basis of any education."[18]

Needless to say, Soka educational institutions are not a place for the teaching of religious doctrine. Yet it is based on a solid and, I believe, universal worldview. If I were to express this in a single phrase, it would be the spirit of shared commitment between teacher and learner, mentor and disciple.

Just as a diamond can be polished only by another diamond, it is only through intense human interaction engaging the entire personality that people can forge themselves, raising themselves up to ever greater heights. It is the relationship between teacher and learner, between mentor and disciple, that makes this possible.

The Lotus Sutra, which contains the essence of Eastern philosophy, expresses the Buddha's determination to make his disciples "equal to me, without any distinction between us."[19] This is the teacher's vow and pledge to raise the learners' life states to the same level as the teacher.

In terms of the essential capacities and possibilities of life, there is no inherent difference between teacher and learner. The mentor creatively and imaginatively uses various means and methods to inspire and awaken in the learner the wisdom and power that has been realized by the teacher. The true teacher, the mentor, desires nothing so much as to be equaled—no, to be exceeded and surpassed—by the students and disciples.

Makiguchi and Toda dedicated, risked, and offered their lives to the goal of awakening individuals to the infinite possibilities of their own lives, enabling them to experience and live out those possibilities in reality.

During World War II, Makiguchi critiqued the core philosophical basis of the militarist authorities of Japan. As a result, he was arrested and died in prison. Toda likewise struggled against and survived the ordeal of imprisonment. Emerging from prison, he dedicated his entire life and being to spreading a philosophy of humanism and working for the happiness of people.

Inheriting this legacy from my mentors I have, as a disciple, founded Soka University of America to be a bastion of profound spirituality.

The Future Is Yours

I have touched on a variety of points, but in conclusion I would like to emphasize that the true value of a university is determined by its graduates. The activities and contributions of its graduates are what establish the worth and standing of a university.

Among the many educators I have had the opportunity to meet is Dean Lawrence E. Carter (1941–) of Morehouse College, which is, of course, the alma mater of Martin Luther King Jr (1929–68). When I asked Dean Carter what is the most important point of pride in the university's history, he answered without hesitation: Our great alumni.

It is the graduates who determine the value of a university. The challenge of a university is to foster as many people as possible who truly contribute to the flourishing of society and the welfare of humankind.

I have twice had the privilege of meeting and sharing thoughts with President David P. Roselle (1939–) of the University of Delaware.

The University of Delaware was established in 1743, several decades before the American colonies declared their independence. The founder, Francis Alison (1705–79), was a young man in his thirties. The first graduating class consisted of just ten people. Facilities, buildings, and textbooks were entirely inadequate; the founder's home served as the main classroom.

And yet from this initial group came state governors, members of Congress, doctors, lawyers, and scholars. Among the first graduating class were three signers of the Declaration of Independence and one signer of the United States Constitution.

When I asked President Roselle what he thought Alison had left to the University of Delaware, his response was clear: Alison's greatest legacy was the students of the first graduating class.

I share his feelings completely. You, the graduates who now take limitless flight into the vast skies of the future, are my greatest legacy to humankind, humanity's greatest treasure.

There were ten members of the first graduating class of the University of Delaware. There are some one hundred members of SUA's Class of 2005. Just imagine the brilliant new world you can create!

I hope that you, who are my very life, will pursue your respective paths of mission, exercising leadership in your places of work and in society, becoming leaders for peace, culture, and justice, leaders of humanity dedicated to the welfare of the people.

Please advance victoriously toward lives of such greatness that future generations will gratefully declare that the first graduating class of SUA opened and forged the path to a new world. I fully believe in and look forward to your victory.

José Ortega y Gasset, the philosopher I referred to earlier, declared, "To live is, in fact, to have dealings with the world: to address oneself to it, exert oneself in it, and occupy oneself with it."[20]

The main stage of your activities awaits you. As global citizens who view the entire globe as your home, I hope you will work for humanity and make vibrant contributions.

Always holding in your hearts the pride of being members of the first graduating class of SUA, please triumph over whatever storms and challenges await you. Please become truly first-rate people in your respective fields of endeavor. To the very end, tread the path in life that will enable you to confidently declare your own victory.

With my entire being I call out: Soka University of America! Become a bastion of hope for world peace! Become the cradle in which is fostered a global civilization of reverence for life!

Creating new value—creating peace and hope for humankind—this is the vast and noble mission borne by each of you as you set out from SUA.

In closing, I would like to offer you these words of Jules Michelet (1798–1874), the French historian, which he addressed to students: "Youth! You bear responsibility for the future. The world needs you!"[21]

Again, my heartfelt congratulations on your graduation!

I salute the glorious first graduating class! I wish you victory and happiness! Together let us create a new era of the victory of Soka education!

Congratulations!

part three:

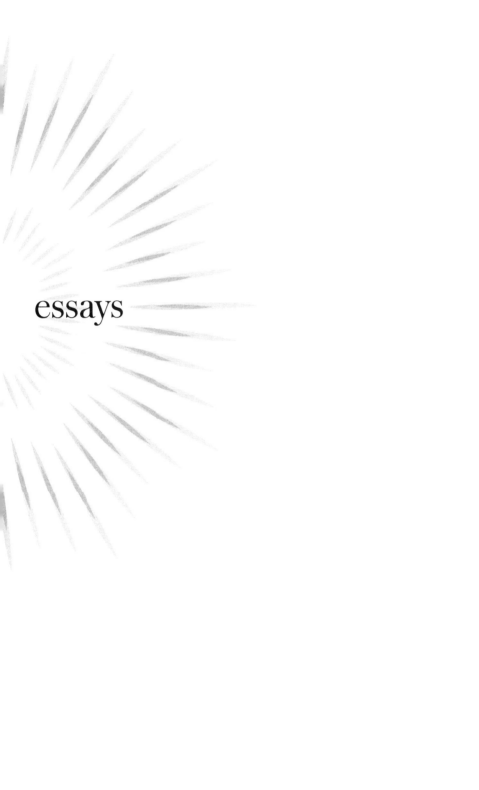

essays

The Tradition of Soka University

March 15, 1998.

SOON WE WILL be greeted by the smiling faces of the cherry blossoms.

Tens of thousands of brilliant and talented young graduates have already passed through the gates of Soka University, citadel of wisdom and intellect, on their way to the twenty-first century. Just the other day, I heard the news that 162 Soka University students (including distance learning students) passed the prefectural teacher employment examinations for 1998. I cannot express how happy, as founder, this makes me.

In recent years, because of the economic downturn and lackluster performance of the business sector, the number of applicants for the exam has risen. Birthrates, however, continue to decline; fewer school-age children means fewer new teachers hired. Despite the intense competition, each year for seven years more than a hundred Soka University students have passed the exam.

This remarkable record of achievement has drawn the admiration and praise of people throughout Japan. I would like to congratulate the students on their indomitable spirit. At the same time, I would like to express my profound gratitude to their teachers and university staff members who have encouraged and supported them.

Starting with Soka University's first graduating class [Class of 1975] to the present, more than twenty-four hundred graduates have secured employment as teachers in public and private schools. I'm sure this would delight Tsunesaburo Makiguchi (1871–1944), the father of value-creating education.

* * *

Education, because it shapes future leaders, is our most crucial undertaking.

In the spring of 1930, Makiguchi wrote in a letter to a friend: "Recent educational policies as well as classroom teachers have become completely bureaucratic and listless, destroying the whole purpose of education. This places Japan's future in grave peril."

The decline of education brings the moral and spiritual decline of the nation's citizens and of society itself. That is why Makiguchi called for educational reform and desired more than anything to foster outstanding educators.

On November 18 of the year he wrote that letter, Makiguchi, together with Josei Toda (1900–58), founded the Soka Kyoiku Gakkai or Value-Creating Education Society.

Makiguchi believed that the purpose of education is to enable children to live lives of happiness. The vision he cherished of the kind of teacher who would carry out that sacred task is not of someone who sits ensconced on the throne of learning as an object of veneration but rather of a public servant who guides those aspiring to ascend that throne themselves.

His was the revolutionary cry of human education.

* * *

Makiguchi often shared this vision with his family members: "In the future, there will be a school system that puts the methods of value-creating education into practice. It will span kindergarten to university level. Young Toda will see to it that my work is carried on."

And Toda said to me, his disciple, "Daisaku, let's establish a university, Soka University. I hope this can be achieved in my lifetime, but that may not be possible. Should that be the case, Daisaku, I'm counting on you to do it. Let's make it the best university in the world!" This was in the late autumn of 1950. At the time, Toda's business ventures were in dire straits. And yet he retained the ability to gaze serenely into the distant future.

I consider education to be the culminating undertaking of my life. Unlike Makiguchi and Toda, who were both teachers, I never studied as a teacher nor taught in the classroom. Nevertheless, I have established the Soka educational system and promoted the ideals and principles of value-creating education throughout the world. That has been my mission as their disciple. In this way I have been able to realize the wish of my noble mentors and predecessors.

Makiguchi's authoritative statement of his educational ideals, *Soka kyoikugaku taikei* (The System of Value-Creating Pedagogy), has so far been translated into four languages. This is the cause of immense joy. And in both Brazil and the United States, a number of schools have incorporated Makiguchi's ideas into the teaching curriculum, all producing remarkable results. The students are excited about their studies, and grades have improved. In Brazil, the theory of value-creating education has gained particularly widespread public acceptance. In 1995, there was one school using this method; today [just three years later] there are eighteen.

We are facing a worldwide educational crisis, and over the years Makiguchi's educational ideas have come to shine as a counterbalancing source of hope, a lifeline in the darkness.

* * *

In what has become a school tradition, I have over the years received many bound volumes of essays written by Soka University students upon graduation. They include essays from students from the very first graduating class through to those of recent years. There are some two-dozen volumes all told. I keep them close to hand and continue to pray for the growth and happiness of each graduate. I frequently go through the essays, asking after their authors; I may send a book, a short message, or a poem to encourage them. For me, each of the graduates is a precious individual, a student who chose to study at the university I founded. The bond we share is one forged through the vows made in our respective youths.

The university is also continuing to develop its international outreach: many Soka University students go to Soka University of America (SUA) in Calabasas, California, for short-term language study programs and to experience life abroad. The day when SUA's Aliso Viejo campus will open is fast approaching. Soka University is to date involved in exchange programs with sixty-seven universities around the globe.

I feel that an "all-star cast" is now assembling for a grand performance on the stage of the twenty-first century.

The Dawn of a Century
of Human Education

January 1, 2000.

We must make whole men, *whole* men . . . .[1]
—VICTOR HUGO (1802–85)

Produce great Persons, the rest follows.[2]
—WALT WHITMAN (1819–92)

SEVERAL YEARS BEFORE Soka University was opened, young men and women came together to help clear the land that was to be the site for the university's first buildings. Tree stumps still protruded here and there from the barren ground. These young people had come from around Japan, filled with a desire to contribute in some way to the new school. They were drenched in perspiration, and their hands were blistered and bleeding from the hard manual work. Envisioning talented students pursuing their studies here in the future, they were focused single-mindedly on the task with no thought of gaining anything in return. Some local members of the Soka Gakkai supported the young people in their efforts by bringing them rice balls and refreshments.

Most of these volunteers never had an opportunity to attend university themselves. I hope that no one involved with Soka University will ever forget that the school was created in this way through the contributions and support of countless ordinary citizens, that it is a university founded by the people. I believe that a university's mission should be to serve people who, much as they might have wished, have not themselves been able to receive higher education.

The Flame of Soka

My part in the founding of Soka University began in the cafeteria of Nihon University in Tokyo's Kanda area in 1950. I was there with my mentor, Josei Toda (1900–58). It was late autumn and the biting cold deepened with each passing day. These were dark, even desperate times.

Three months earlier, the credit association run by Toda had been ordered to suspend operations. Every day, angry creditors besieged his office, cursing us and demanding payment. They hurled groundless allegations, accusations, and threats at us. Some even harassed Toda at his home from the early hours of the morning. The odds seemed overwhelmingly stacked against us.

One by one, employees began leaving the company. Toda was exhausted and haggard. I, too, was tired to the bone from fighting a solitary battle in the effort to protect and support my mentor. My exhaustion was so deep that at times my body would refuse to obey me.

But during this period, Toda would take advantage of any lull in our activities to share with me his future visions and goals. It was all too clear to me—it was a solemn, indisputable reality—that he wanted me to carry on his work should something happen to him. And it was so on that day in Kanda.

Sitting in the cafeteria, he was discussing theories of national identity and economic trends, when he broached the idea of founding a university.

"Daisaku, let's establish a university, Soka University. I hope this can be achieved in my lifetime, but that may not be possible. Should that be the case, Daisaku, I'm counting on you to do it." In that instant, a bright flame, the dream of Soka University, was kindled in my heart.

To others, my mentor and I must have presented a destitute sight. In truth, Toda could not pay my wages, and I could not afford a warm overcoat even though winter was quickly closing in. Had we spoken to others of starting a university, they would surely have ridiculed us and dismissed the idea out of hand. But in our hearts, my mentor and I were kings. Toda declared, "Let's make it the best university in the world!" On that day, the flame of Soka University that burned fiercely in his heart was passed on to me.

The flame within Toda had been lit by his mentor, the Soka Gakkai's founder, Tsunesaburo Makiguchi (1871–1944), who once said to him, "In the future, we must found a school based on the value-creating [*soka*] pedagogy that I have been formulating. If we can't do it during my lifetime, please do it in yours." On another occasion, he expressed his confidence that "young Toda will build Soka University without fail."

Understanding Makiguchi's fervent wish more than anyone, but now finding himself in dire financial circumstances that left even the next day uncertain, Toda suffered deep pain and mental anguish. Thus, his words to me bore the weight of a final testament.

Around this same period, the Japanese minister of education, Teiyu Amano (1884–1980) expressed the opinion that the fundamental pillar of any educational reform had to be a clear determination to realize what he termed *human revolution*.[3] Maybe because this idea wasn't underpinned by a solid philosophical foundation, or because of the competing interests of politicians, bureaucrats, and big business, this lofty ideal was soon forgotten, and the effects of this are evident throughout present-day Japanese society.

The Goal of Education

When deadlocked, return to your starting point—this was Makiguchi's creed.

Writing in the 1930s, the Soka Gakkai's founder expressed his deep concern that education in Japan seemed either to consist of empty abstraction—with scholars who lacked actual teaching experience importing new theories from the West and imposing these on classroom teachers—or to be designed to instill narrow-minded and intolerant nationalism.

Subservience to the tyranny of borrowed ideas or subservience to political authority—both demonstrate a lack of moral courage; neither expresses the courage and conviction of independent thought.

But more than anything, Makiguchi felt that the essential goal of children's happiness had been forgotten. Where, he demanded, was the love for children?

In his view, those who called most loudly for children to receive proper moral guidance and direction were the ones most in need of such guidance themselves. His critique of their intellectual and moral failings was scathing.

Makiguchi used the allegory of medical treatment to make his point. If a physician prescribes the wrong treatment, he can kill the patient. Mistaken education can be equally deadly. While the results may not be as immediately apparent as the effects of the mistaken treatment of a medical condition, the negative impact will become undeniable with the passage of decades. Japan's present course, Makiguchi warned, would result in ruin.

His cry, however, was coldly ignored. Most educational professionals found it presumptuous for a "mere elementary school principal" to propose new pedagogical theories. Their response was an essentially emotional reaction. It reflected the prevailing arrogance and condescension toward the common people and anything born from among the common people.

What use are universities if all they produce are individuals who look down on their fellow citizens? It was just such overweening elites that plunged Japan and its Asian neighbors into the hell of militarism. In complete contrast, what burned in Makiguchi's heart was a profound love for children—a love so intense that he wrote of feeling truly unbearable anguish at the thought of their suffering.

Neither Makiguchi, a great scholar who bequeathed to his disciple the mission of building a university, nor the disciple, Toda, were themselves university professors. Rather, they devoted themselves to the most fundamental stage of education, that of teaching elementary school children.

In the cold northern island of Hokkaido where Makiguchi lived before he moved to Tokyo in 1900, he would wash students' chapped hands with warm water in winter to ease the pain. When snow storms raged outside, he would carry young students home on his back.

The Mikasa Elementary School in Tokyo, where he served as principal for several years in the 1920s, was located in one of the city's most impoverished precincts. Broken windowpanes could not be repaired; instead they were covered with paper. Many children worked during the day to support their families, and evening classes were established to meet their needs. By the dim light of gas lanterns, they studied arithmetic and other subjects, fighting exhaustion and sleepiness.

For students who were too poor to bring packed lunches

from home, Makiguchi would spend part of his salary to provide meals and snacks. He would place the food in the caretaker's room for the children to collect, so they wouldn't have to suffer unnecessary attention or humiliation.

Children's sorrows and chagrins—for not being able to go to school or study, for living in poverty, for enduring bleak home lives—Makiguchi and Toda understood them all.

The willingness to do whatever is needed, the clear understanding that teachers exist to help all children, without exception, become happy: the pedagogy of value creation was born from the spiritual light of compassion and love for humanity. This is why it has found a reception among educators around the world.

And this is why it was inevitable that it would clash head-on with the wartime educational policies of militarist Japan—a society rife with discrimination, a land whose heart was closed to the rest of the world.

I have exerted myself to give form to the vision of Soka University. I have written ceaselessly, making financial contributions from the royalties. I have striven to win the cooperation and trust of many people. I have visited dozens of universities throughout the world. When typhoons hit Tokyo, my foremost thought is for the safety of the university. When I hear of students becoming ill, I send messages of encouragement. It is not my intent here to stress my own efforts—everything I have done has been motivated by the desire that the students be victorious in their lives.

While I am delighted by such developments as the completion of the university's new Central Tower, what delights me far more is seeing a grand tower of victory being built in the depths of each student's life.

Holding aloft the flame that has been cherished by the succession of mentor and disciple of Soka—the light to which we have devoted our lives—please build magnificent, triumphant treasure towers of human education in your respective spheres of mission.

This year, 2000, marks the centennial of Josei Toda's birth. It is a momentous turning point. Material and social revolutions were the struggles of the twentieth century, while the revolution of humanity itself will be the challenge of the twenty-first. As we move from the darkness of the end of the old century into the dawn of the new, there is no mistaking what needs to be done.

> We must send the sparks flying
> from the hearts of youth
> using the flame within.
> To educate is to kindle the soul's flame!

Teachers of My Childhood

From the book One by One *by Daisaku Ikeda, published in 2004.*

WHEN SPRING ARRIVES, heaven and earth, towns and cities—everything—takes on a new brightness. The fresh faces of the students just starting school as the cherry blossoms burst into bloom are also bright and shining.

Although many people delight in the beautiful blossoms, few bother to consider the roots that make that blossoming possible. In life, our roots are largely formed by our first experience of education, the years we spend in elementary school.

"Blooming, blooming, the cherry trees are blooming . . ." I remember my very first school textbook when I entered elementary school in the spring of 1934. Opening it with excitement, I saw a beautiful spring scene of cherry trees in bloom. In the distance there were mountains, and in the foreground the lovely pink cherry blossoms. This book, titled *Shogaku kokugo tokuhon* (An Elementary School Reader) was the first textbook in Japan to be printed in color; it had just come into use the year before I started school.

"Blooming, blooming"—our teacher wrote the words in big letters on the blackboard. Miss Tejima was tall and slim. Many people, I would imagine, retain a clear memory of their elementary school teachers. I, too, recall Miss Tejima with great clarity—the color of her clothing, her hairstyle, and even her characteristic gestures. On one occasion, Miss Tejima selected me and just one other student from our entire school year and praised our compositions, saying that they were very well written. I was a little embarrassed to be singled out, but I was also very pleased. Everyone is happy when praised sincerely. It builds confidence. Indeed, Miss Tejima's praise may well have influenced my desire to become a writer.

Changing Times

I attended Haneda Elementary School No. 2 in Tokyo, which at the time was a two-story wooden building surrounded by rice paddies. On frosty winter days, the water in the paddies sometimes froze. On such days, a rowdy band of children, we would stray off the road and, shouting "This way! This way!" cut through the paddies on our way to school. It was a tranquil, idyllic time.

But things were changing quickly. Japan was entering a dark, oppressive period in its history. The Manchurian Incident, which began Japan's invasion of China, took place when I was three. When I was four, there was an abortive coup d'état in which the prime minister was assassinated, and when I was five, Japan withdrew from the League of Nations. Young as we were, we didn't understand what was going on in the world, but the rising waves of the troubled times reached even into our classrooms. A few pages after the blooming cherries in our reader was a page with the barking command: "Advance! Advance! Soldier, advance!"

Another spring came around, and once more the season of cherry blossoms arrived. About this time, my father suffered an attack of debilitating rheumatism and became bedridden. We were forced to scale back our family business of seaweed processing; our lives grew harder day by day. My eldest brother had enjoyed good grades, but he was forced to quit school and go to work to contribute to the family finances.

In the third and fourth grades, I had my first male teacher, Mr. Takeuchi. He had just graduated from teachers college and was young and energetic. He placed a particularly heavy emphasis on physical education: "You can be as smart as you like, but if you don't build a strong body when you're young, you'll be of no use to anyone as an adult. Health is important. Study is important. True education combines both." This appears to have been his credo as a teacher.

I was on the short side and not very strong, so it was no easy thing to meet Mr. Takeuchi's expectations. To this day, I am moved whenever I remember how keenly he encouraged me to develop my physical strength and become healthy. I also remember how he taught us about the meaning of the Olympics, explaining in detail how they were conducted. That was in 1936, the year the Berlin Olympics were held in Germany. Mr. Takeuchi stressed the importance of holding the Olympics on a grand scale every four years as a means of promoting world peace.

He clearly hated war. In the depths of his heart I think that he strongly opposed the militaristic trend of the times, believing in the importance of peace and encouraging children to grow into fine individuals with a true love of peace.

Watching Over Growth

In Japan, people who tend and care for cherry trees are called *sakuramori,* a word that implies a sense of careful stewardship. The *sakuramori* look after the cherry trees, encouraging them to grow, tending to their welfare, and generally caring for them throughout the four seasons. The care they extend expresses faith in the power of life as it grows and develops into the future. They don't fuss too much about the trees, but at the same time they never ignore them. They observe the trees' growth in great detail but allow them to develop freely. For example, if we stake a tree from the very beginning, the tree will rely on the stakes for support and not grow strong on its own.

The roots are especially important. One expert on trees says that the spread of the crown of a cherry tree is mirrored almost exactly by the spread of its roots below ground. If we water the tree only around the base of the trunk, the tree will become "lazy" and not bother to spread its roots far in search of water.

For people, "roots" correspond to the tenacity of our spirit, our refusal to give up. Once a tree has taken firm root, it can survive even on a rocky mountain face buffeted by powerful winds.

Trees are living things. They are not machines. Every cherry tree is unique. They each grow and thrive in different environments. That is why there is no manual that can tell us how to grow a cherry tree. The only way to succeed is to learn the particular tree's character and idiosyncrasies and, taking them into account, warmly care for it.

Each child is also unique. Each has a distinct way of flowering that is his or hers alone. To raise a tree or to foster people, we need a patient faith in their potential to flourish. A child who has poor grades or who is out of control and behaving badly now may in the future grow into a person who does truly remarkable things. It is not at all rare for a child we think we know very well to suddenly change and show us a side we never would have imagined. To the precise degree that we care for and have faith in children, they will extend and spread their roots. And it is this that will give them the strength to survive and make their way successfully through life.

Protection, as in "protection of the natural environment," assumes that nature is frail and therefore needs our protection. But stewardship expresses a spirit of awe and respect for the potential for limitless growth. I believe that such awe and respect for children should be the foundation of education.

Vivid Memories

My teacher in the fifth and sixth grades was Mr. Hiyama. I think he was about twenty-five or twenty-six at the time. His broad forehead and clear, bright eyes gave an impression of intellect and acuity. His classes were sometimes challenging, but they were always interesting. Between classes he would read Eiji Yoshikawa's (1892–1962) samurai tale *Miyamoto Musashi* (*Musashi: An Epic Novel of the Samurai Musashi*) to us, gesturing and posing and reading with dramatic expression, bringing the story alive. We were pulled entirely into the world portrayed in the novel; we could see Musashi dashing about and rival swordsman Kojiro brandishing his sword right before our eyes. It took a year, but Mr. Hiyama read the novel to us in its entirety.

During one class, he spread out a large world map before us and asked us where we wanted to go. I pointed to the middle of the vast expanse of Asia. "I see!" he said. "You have pointed to Dunhuang. There are many wonderful treasures there." From that moment a fascination with Dunhuang—the oasis city on the silk trade routes famous for its temples and painted grottos—took hold in my mind.

I may have pointed to China because my eldest brother, whom I loved and respected, had been sent there as a soldier.

He was drafted when I was a fourth grader. After him, my next two older brothers were called up for military service.

My father's rheumatism was improving, but with my three brothers away we were short of help, and our family finances got worse and worse. When I was a fifth grader, we had to sell our house and move to a smaller one in the same area. The original house had a large yard with a big pond and a tall cherry tree. Whenever I looked up from beneath the cherry tree in our yard, it seemed as if countless bell-shaped flowers were falling from the bright blue spring sky. It was hard to say goodbye to that big tree, but I was glad that I didn't have to change schools because of the move.

A Teacher's Kindness

Hoping to do what I could to help my family, I got a job delivering newspapers. I woke up each morning while it was still dark and helped out with the seaweed production. When I finished, I delivered my papers and then went to school. After returning from school, I helped with the family business again, pulling the dried sheets of *nori* seaweed off the racks. Then I delivered the evening paper. At night there was the work of cleaning the seaweed, removing any impurities. I look back now on those busy days with fondness.

When I was in sixth grade, we took a school trip to Kansai. We were away for four nights and five days. It was my first trip away from home, and I was very excited. My mother had given me some pocket money, which she had somehow managed to scrape together. I used it to treat my friends, and at the end of the first day it was almost gone. Mr. Hiyama must have been watching me the whole time, because he called to me as I was going up the stairs of the inn where we were staying and said,

"Daisaku, your elder brothers are all away at the war. You have to buy your parents a souvenir from your trip."

I was crushed; of course he was right. My mother's face appeared before my eyes. Smiling, Mr. Hiyama called me downstairs. He placed some money in my palm and closed my fingers around it. I think it was two one-yen bills. At that time, it was a large amount of money. I was happy. I breathed a sigh of relief. When I returned home and gave my mother her gift, I told her what had happened. "You must never forget Mr. Hiyama," she said with a gentle smile.

I don't feel that he was giving me special treatment. He wouldn't have been as well loved as he was by so many students if he were the kind of teacher who had favorites. He cared for us all equally, looking deep into our hearts, aware of the family situations that were the "soil" that nourished us. I will never forget the warm affection with which he looked at each of us during our graduation ceremony, large tears running down his cheeks.

In 1940, I graduated from elementary school and entered Haneda Higher Elementary School. My teacher for the next two years was Mr. Okabe, whom we called "Mr. Buccaneer."

He was from Okayama in the western part of Japan and used to make us laugh by telling us that in a past life he must have been the leader of a pirate crew sailing the Inland Sea, which was near his hometown. He was tall with jet-black hair and a handsome, intelligent face. There were some forty boys in our class—no girls. Mr. Okabe often encouraged me to exercise to strengthen myself physically. He loved sumo wrestling and taught us various sumo techniques. Even though I was small, I did my best. In summer, we would take off our shirts and run to the Tama River to swim.

At first glance, Mr. Okabe appeared very intimidating, but I never felt afraid of him. It may have been because I was rather shy, but I can't remember him ever scolding me. Once, one of the students in our class was hit by another teacher. When Mr. Okabe heard about it he charged into the staff room shouting, "Which one of you hit one of my students?!" He had a very strong sense of right and wrong. He may have seemed gruff on the outside, but we all felt his concern and affection.

Growing Nationalism

When I was in my second year at Haneda Higher Elementary School, its name was changed to Haginaka National People's School. This was mandated by the National People's School Order, a law filled with militaristic overtones that sought to turn children into soldiers. Terms such as *loyal subjects of the Emperor, drilling* and *group training* became staples of school life, and the gymnasiums of many schools were converted into martial arts training halls. Japan was sliding down the slope from war with China into the even more disastrous Pacific War. In their arrogance and stupidity, the leaders of the day had no thought for the welfare of ordinary citizens. They were driving the nation into the abyss of war with a mix of threats and well-crafted slogans.

Life became harder with each passing day, and cherry trees, whose wood burned well, were cut down one after another for fuel. The tree in our old garden that I loved so dearly was cut down, and a factory for military supplies was built where it had stood.

Education has a truly astonishing power to cast a spell over the innocent hearts of children. Many of the students in my class at the new "national people's school" applied to enlist as soldiers or as civilian colonists on the Chinese mainland.

They did this because it seemed to be the highest expression of patriotism: to be a pioneering hero of the new era. I, too, wanted to become a student pilot in the navy after I graduated. Although I was concerned about my family and how they would fare without me, I secretly sent in an application.

"That's Enough!"

I wasn't there when a representative of the navy visited my home. My father sent the man away saying: "My three eldest sons are all in the army. The fourth will be going soon. Do you really plan to take away my fifth as well? No more. That's enough!"

When I got home, my father berated me fiercely. I was never so harshly scolded before or after. It gave me a glimpse of my father's true feelings, which he usually kept to himself.

After graduating, I went to work at the Niigata Steelworks. The war situation had worsened, and there was an intensifying sense of impending defeat. In 1945, the last year of the war, air raids on Tokyo started on New Year's Day. Our days were filled with war and air raids. Even so, when spring arrived, those cherry trees that remained began blossoming, honest and true to their nature as always.

On the night of April 15, when the cherry petals were starting to fall, southern Tokyo was attacked in a massive air raid. The anguished sound of the air-raid sirens wailed, and mighty B-29s appeared like majestic conquerors, flying steady and low across the sky. The staccato of the strafing from the American planes combined with people's screams. Incendiary bombs fell like a heavy rain. Tongues of flame leaped up here and there, burning madly. In an instant, the entire area was a sea of raging fire, and everyone was desperately trying to flee the conflagration. Parents were separated from small children. Sons and daughters struggled in vain to save elderly parents. All those caught up in this hellish nightmare of death and destruction were filled with searing anguish. Even now, it brings unendurable pain to write of that night.

When the sun rose the next morning, the entire area where I lived had been burned to the ground. Except for Haneda Airport, the town had been reduced to ashes. Both my beloved elementary school and the so-called national people's school had been razed.

Around this time, I found myself walking alone, lost in thought. The war dragged on. What would happen to Japan? What would become of my family? How would I live my life? I could not envision a future. Eventually, I found myself in a small section of town that hadn't burned. A little group of cherry trees was in fragrant bloom. It was like a quiet and peaceful dream. In the vast expanse of burned-out gray, the beautiful colors of the cherry trees glowed like a torch. In the midst of so much death, here was the light of shining life. "Blooming, blooming, the cherry trees are blooming. . . ."

Words on a Wall

In those days, even cherry trees were made into symbols of death. The Japanese people were told to be like cherry blossoms, to scatter courageously in the wind without a whisper of regret. But the cherry trees before me clearly rejected such perversion and spoke to me—powerfully, sublimely—of life. They were overflowing with hope.

"Live! Live fully and deeply! Never cease living! Outlive the winter and let your own unique nature bloom," they said to me. Powerful emotions welled up and filled my heart. On the wall of a burned-out factory building, I used a piece of chalk to write a passage from a poem that I composed. Many people carried chalk with them in those days so that in an emergency they could leave a message that would enable their families to find them. I didn't bother signing my poem, but later I saw that others who shared my feelings had written their thoughts below mine on the wall.

A certain poet once wrote: "Blossoms that scatter, blossoms that remain to become blossoms that scatter." I had not scattered but had survived, and was now seventeen. The war had for too long kept me from school and learning. I was filled with the desire to study, to learn, to read books.

I have never forgotten the beloved teachers of my youth. I have stayed in touch with a number of them to this day. Mr. Okabe once wrote to me, exhorting me to live strongly and tenaciously in the face of all obstacles. In another letter he encouraged me, saying, "The taller a tree grows, the harder the wind blows against it; please endure the wind and snow."

I was able to have a reunion with Mr. Hiyama in Tochigi in 1973. He and his wife had traveled an hour and a half by bus to see me. I hadn't seen him for more than thirty years, but he still had the aura of a great educator who had made a fine job of raising many children. "You don't seem to have any time to rest," he said. "Please be careful not to harm your health." His gaze was just as warm and caring as it had been on that school trip long ago.

Sitting in front of him, I felt as if I had returned to my elementary school days. To a student, your teacher is always your teacher, and to a teacher, your students are always your students. How wonderful it is to have a true teacher! It is easy to encounter a teacher who imparts knowledge but hard to encounter one who teaches you how to live.

Elementary education is the most critical. But how should we teach elementary school students? It is a very difficult job. That is precisely why I have such tremendous respect for elementary school teachers who do succeed in this challenging work. Are high school teachers more important than elementary school teachers? Are university professors more important than high school teachers? Absolutely not. It is just this kind of erroneous thinking that afflicts our society today: theorists often have the mistaken idea that they are better than practitioners.

Fostering the Future

An architect who theorizes about architecture is in no way superior to a carpenter who can actually build a house. An agricultural expert is not more productive than a farmer who actually grows vegetables or rice. I sometimes think there are too many people who theorize about things and far too few who actually make painstaking efforts to achieve something.

There are many people who love cherries and other flowering trees but few who truly appreciate the efforts of those who work behind the scenes to keep the trees alive and healthy. The life of an educator is also far from glamorous. Teaching is inconspicuous work that doesn't get much attention; it's a matter of continuous hard work and effort. But it is precisely because of such teachers dedicated to fostering the future that the next generation of children can grow up straight and strong. We must never forget this crucially important fact.

In those dark days, when the power of ultranationalist authorities pressed down so heavily on Japanese society, my teachers held up for their students the great light of humanity. Just like teachers today who are earnestly committed to their profession, they firmly embraced their students and shared their lives with them, while struggling against the intrusions of political power into the realm of education.

If being blessed with good teachers is one of life's joys, there can be no one happier than I.

Soka Women's College—A Shining Citadel of Women's Education

December 8, 2003.

Soka Women's College—
the youthful foundation
for lifelong victory.

OPENING THE CLASSROOM door, I was welcomed by the dazzling smiles and cheerful greetings of the young women inside. On October 1, 2002, I visited Room 101 at Soka Women's College [a two-year junior college located on the campus of Soka University] in Hachioji, Tokyo, during the second period of the day.

College president Katsuhiko Fukushima, who was accompanying me, suggested that I take this rare opportunity of a class visit to speak with the students, and with the kind permission of Dr. Tadashi Kanai, the class's lecturer and dean of academic affairs, I talked a little on the topics of learning, life, and happiness. [See p. 133 for the text of the author's speech that day.]

I selected as my subject matter the novel *A Life* by French writer Guy de Maupassant (1850–93), which depicts the tale of one woman's life from her late teens through to old age. I hoped it would afford an opportunity to discuss with these students—who were spearheading the way to the Century of Women—the philosophy for leading truly victorious lives.

I began by noting that "it is in scaling life's mountains, crossing life's valleys, and traversing life's precipitous peaks, ever advancing with integrity and fortitude, that happiness is found." I wished to engrave a genuine understanding of life, transcending merely abstract or superficial perspectives, in the students' hearts. The great French writer and philosopher Jean-Jacques Rousseau (1712–78) declared that there is no true happiness without genuine wisdom or good sense.[1]

I said to the gathered young women, whom I treasured as if they were my own beloved daughters: "Out in society, there are many different kinds of people: malicious people who seek to undermine and deceive others; arrogant people who scorn and despise others. We study so that we can prevail over such people, succeed in all our endeavors, and lead fulfilling lives."

Some students nodded in agreement with my words, their eyes sparkling with intelligence; others took careful notes. Time and again, happy, unrestrained laughter rippled through the room. It was a scene that perfectly depicted the observation of French thinker Simone Weil (1909–43): "Intelligence only grows and bears fruit in joy. The joy of learning is as indispensable to study as breathing is to runners."[2]

My wife sat smiling gently as she looked on in one corner of the room.

* * *

How beautiful the hearts
of the students
of Soka Women's College.

I first proposed the idea of establishing Soka Women's College in July 1969. As a prelude, the Kansai Soka Girls Junior and Senior High Schools opened in Katano, outside of Osaka, four years later, in 1973. With the future aim of launching a women's college in mind, we set about building an exemplary tradition in women's education.

In 1982, reflecting on the changing times and after careful consideration, it was decided to make the Soka high schools in both Kansai and Tokyo [the latter of which had been a boys' school] coeducational institutions. I remained committed, however, to the establishment of a special college for women that would bring a fresh, invigorating light to shine in the cold, impersonal, dog-eat-dog atmosphere of Japanese society.

Our great teacher of value-creating education, Tsunesaburo Makiguchi (1871–1944), firmly believed that women would be the builders of the ideal society of the future. At the dawn of the twentieth century, he was one of the first in Japan to initiate correspondence education courses specially designed for women. In that respect, Soka Women's College would also signal a fruition of Makiguchi's vision to provide specialized education for women.

We decided that Soka Women's College would open its doors in time to receive students graduating from the first coeducational classes of the Soka high schools. It was on April 9, 1985—the campus abloom with cherry blossoms—that Soka Women's College, an institution committed to nurturing the shining potential of each student, held its first entrance ceremony. A total of 373 bright, high-spirited members of the first class, each with a brilliant mission, gathered in the college's brand-new Swan Gymnasium. The emerald green scarves my wife and I had presented to each student—a gift to celebrate their entrance to the school—stood out vividly against their pristine white blouses.

In my heart, I joined my palms together in a gesture of reverence and said to all of them, "Thank you for coming to the junior college I have founded." My wife and I had spoken of how we would always do everything we could to support the students of Soka Women's College as if they were our own daughters.

The flowering trees and shrubs that adorned the grounds around the school's buildings—red- and white-flowering plums, cherries, peaches, paulownia, pomegranates, and Japanese bush clover, to name but a few—had been planted at my suggestion.

I attended the celebratory events to mark the school's opening—held over two days, before the entrance ceremony—greeting the distinguished guests who had been invited, including representatives of major firms and businesses. I handed out my name card and bowed deeply, saying: "In two years, our first class will graduate. Please keep them in mind." I wished to do everything possible to pave the way for the bright futures for all these young women, and I am happy to report that the employment rate of Soka Women's College graduates is nearly 100 percent every year.

*　*　*

In conjunction with the school's founding, I presented the students with three mottoes: (1) Be a person of intelligence, happiness, and virtue; (2) Be a person of principle, working for harmony for all; and (3) Be a person with a global view and social wisdom.

Today, there are over sixty-five hundred Soka Women's College graduates who have made these mottoes their guiding principles in life as they continue to blaze a trail toward the Century of Women. They have a high reputation in society for excellence, and leaders in every field have expressed their trust and admiration for them. Nothing could make me happier. Graduates of the junior college are pursuing careers in a wide variety of areas. They range from accountants to scholars, teachers, and executive secretaries in major firms, as well as the founders of their own businesses. Others are flight attendants for international carriers or conductors on Japan's high-speed bullet train. A number of refreshing new political leaders are also now emerging from their ranks.

In every field and profession, Soka Women's College graduates are shining brightly as leaders dedicated to the welfare of others and society as a whole.

Our most fundamental goal is peace, and Soka Women's College prides itself on fostering a steady stream of women leaders committed to this goal.

A Buddhist scripture strictly warns: "In the case of a woman, if jealousy piles up, she will turn into a poisonous snake."[3] It is important not to be defeated by one's inner weakness or negativity. Peace is born from a pure heart. The true emissary of peace lives in the beautiful hearts of women who love and cherish life and delight in others' happiness as if it were their own.

I have been told that Wellesley College, one of the leading academic institutions for women in the United States, is also committed to providing an education for women who will take leadership for world peace. When I met with Wellesley's dean of religious and spiritual life, Victor Kazanjian, he stressed the importance of injecting spiritual and religious depth into the learning process. I am in complete agreement with this point.

When the first class at Soka Women's College announced they would like to hold a student festival in the autumn of that first year, I suggested the name Swan Festival. This idea was greeted with delight and approval.

Graduates of the college—members of the alumnae association known as the Swan Alumnae—have embarked out into the wide world, their efforts to bring people's hearts together creating a shimmering rainbow of peace.

* * *

Swan Alumnae
endure, and take flight
to the citadel of happiness.

The students of Soka Women's College have many opportunities to come into contact with people of outstanding character and intellect from around the globe.

In December 1992, Rosa Parks (1913–2005), a pivotal figure of the American Civil Rights Movement, spoke at what was then the Soka University Los Angeles (SULA) campus. Students from the college who were participating in a short-term, intensive language program there welcomed Mrs. Parks and performed the song "Mother" as an expression of their admiration and respect for her. Mrs. Parks, wreathed in smiles, said she was deeply moved by the young women's purity of heart. This event opened the way for the friendship that my wife and I later formed with Mrs. Parks.

During a discussion with the Soka Women's College students, Mrs. Parks shared that one of the people she most respects and admires is her mother, because the latter taught her from childhood to be strong and to uphold her personal dignity.

Women have an innate capacity to teach and pass on to the next generation the importance of respect for human dignity and the sanctity of life. The Century of Women will be an age when women, as mothers, teachers, and role models, will demonstrate this capacity to the fullest. As a result, the Century of Women will also be a century of education—which, in turn, will make it a true century of peace.

* * *

Swan Alumnae
soaring high
on the wings of victory.

A bronze statue of the renowned scientist Marie Curie (1867– 1934) stands on the campus of Soka Women's College, gazing down at the young women studying there.

During Curie's youth, her homeland Poland was under harsh foreign rule. Outraged by the social injustices that were being perpetrated, she called out, "I can bear an insult, and even forgive it, if someone does it to me only, but I could never forgive an offence to [my homeland]!"[4] Wishing to be a force for change, she resolved to study hard and become a person of great capability. In the midst of her youthful struggles, she declared proudly, "First principle: never to let one's self be beaten down by persons or by events."[5] And true to her word, she lived a life of victory.

Curie endured the all too untimely death of her beloved husband. She refused to let verbal abuse motivated by envy and malice get the better of her. She insisted proudly and fearlessly that to violate the human rights of those who work with a noble sense of mission for people's happiness is a crime. In a letter of encouragement to her daughter, she wrote: "We will continue to have courage. We must cherish the firm hope that sunny skies await us after the rain."[6]

Her statue, depicting her standing with a laboratory flask in hand, continually calls on students to exhibit invincible courage and hope.

* * *

Jane Addams (1860–1935), the celebrated social activist who was the first American woman to receive the Nobel Peace Prize (in 1931), made a pledge with her fellow students at the girls' boarding school she attended. She recounts that they vowed eternal allegiance to their early ideals and warned one another against the perils of becoming entrenched in self-centered ways.[7] These vows that Addams made with her friends, I feel, have much in common with the lofty bonds of friendship shared by the students of Soka Women's College.

Incidentally, Soka Ikeda College of Arts and Science for Women, in Chennai, India—of which I am honorary founder and my wife is honorary principal—will conduct its first graduation ceremony for its first graduating class in January 2004.

Our Swan Alumnae members have sisters throughout Japan and the world who embrace the same ideals and goals as they do. I am confident that their heart-to-heart network of shared commitment will steadily expand to become a magnificent foundation for peace.

The two years that students spend at Soka Women's College may be brief, but those few short years of their youth can give rise to a precious treasure of the heart infused with ten or twenty years' worth of learning. The training, education, and friendships we acquire in our youth can serve as a source of strength and inspiration for the rest of our lives.

From April 2004, Soka Women's College will make a fresh departure with extensive overhauls to its two departments, which have been renamed the Modern Business Department and the English Communications Department. And in 2005, the college will celebrate its twentieth anniversary. Construction work on a new Asakaze Dormitory for boarding students is also progressing steadily.

The time has come for the students of Soka Women's College, the "swans of Soka," to set forth into the unbounded skies of the twenty-first century—their own century of happiness and peace.

> With bright confidence and hope,
> may you, the pioneers
> of the Century of Women,
> each without exception,
> adorn your lives with victory!

part four:

brief thoughts

Education Above All

ALL THE WORLD LEADERS with whom I have spoken agree that education is absolutely fundamental to human happiness, social prosperity, and world peace. In the search for social development and reform, concentrating exclusively on the political and economic dimension is bound to lead to an impasse, as indeed it has already done. All serious thinkers have come to the conclusion that, though it may seem indirect, education is the surest way.[1]

* * *

The path of education is one of continuous trailblazing. As long as there is misery in the world, we must never cease our efforts in that regard. Indeed, the true purpose and mission of education is to overcome human suffering.

Life is short. The most valuable thing we can devote our lives to is fostering people who will build a new age for the sake of tomorrow.[2]

* * *

Education makes us free. The world of knowledge and of the intellect is where all people can meet and converse. Education liberates people from prejudice. It frees the human heart from its violent passions. It is education that severs the dark fetters of ignorance about the laws that govern the universe.

Finally, it is through education that we are liberated from

powerlessness, from the burden of mistrust directed against
ourselves. To awaken the abilities that have been lying dormant within. To arouse and extend the soul's aspiration to
become full and complete. Can there be any more sublime
experience in life?[3]

* * *

Education does not mean coercing people to fit one rigid
and unvaried mold; this is mere ideological indoctrination.
Rather, it represents the most effective means of fostering the
positive potential inherent in all people—self-restraint, empathy for others, and the unique personality and character of
each person. To do this, education must be a personal, even
spiritual, encounter and interaction between human beings,
between teacher and learner.

The teachings of Buddhism employ the analogy of flowering fruit trees—cherry, plum, peach, and damson—each
blossoming and bearing fruit in its own unique way, to express
the value of diversity. Each living thing, in other words, has
a distinct character, individuality, and purpose in this world.
Accordingly, people should develop their own unique capabilities as they work to build a world of cooperation where all
people acknowledge both their differences and their fundamental equality, a world where a rich diversity of peoples and
cultures is nourished, each enjoying respect and harmony.[4]

* * *

Respect for human life must be the foundation of all education. The dignity and uniqueness of life is inherent in individual personalities and in the entire human race. Humanity
depends on the natural world; when we respect humanity, we
must revere and learn from nature. Recognizing the dignity of

the individual must result in mutual recognition and respect: recognizing the absolute fundamental dignity of human life brings diverse values to flower by encouraging people everywhere to learn from each other on an equal footing.[5]

* * *

Today education generally strives exclusively to force students into molds useful to industrial society, whereas, by its very nature, it ought to enable each student to fulfil their diverse potential.[6]

Teachers Are of Prime Importance

The personal growth of the actual protagonists and agents of education—teachers—is the foundation for the revitalization of education.

In the school setting, teachers play a major role in the educational environment for students. The interaction that takes place between educators and students, this life-to-life communication, is the true starting point of education.

It is also teachers, involved as they are on the front lines of education, who are most aware of problems in educational policies and who can make the most difference in affecting change in those areas.

All of this makes the educator's self-transformation and philosophy on life, education and humanity critical factors in effectively reforming education.[7]

* * *

Everyone has the power to create value. The question is how to tap this power. The proper environment must be created.

In the classroom, teachers are of prime importance. More

than anything else, teachers' abilities determine whether education will succeed or fail. They need to share with and pass on to students the inner spiritual qualities they have acquired. Only through communication on this profound level can students discover their own enormous powers, awaken to them, and act with vitality and vigor. This process is the quintessence of human education.[8]

* * *

Even if someone gains position and wealth, it does not necessarily guarantee that they will be happy. At the same time, even if someone seems to be happy, there is no telling how long that happiness will last. True happiness is something we create for ourselves from this present moment and where we are right now, irrespective of our circumstances.

Makiguchi believed that children's happiness depends upon fostering their ability to create value. In other words, children need to develop the ability to open the way forward for themselves and advance freely in any direction.

How admirable are the daily efforts of teachers to draw forth from each of their students the ability to create value, which is also the ability to create happiness![9]

Each Child Should Be Respected

It is also true that the home is not always a safe environment for children. We hear of cases in which vulnerable children from such homes seek out children weaker than themselves and bully them. This represents a chain reaction of abuse and bullying, in which the negative emotional states of adults overwhelmed by reality are mirrored in their children.

It is imperative to create a society that serves the essential needs of education, where children's happiness is the guiding principle. To do so, we must build a network that will protect our children—one that encompasses schools, families, communities, and policymakers.

What I mean by a society that serves the essential needs of education is one where, above all, children's voices can be heard. Only when society listens to and responds to the voices of its youngest members can adults and children alike enjoy peace and happiness. The pursuit of children's happiness is ultimately linked to the joy and fulfillment of adults.[10]

* * *

One of the underlying causes that often gives rise to bullying is the impulse to reject those who are different. That's why it is all the more crucial for teachers and students alike to value each person's individuality and to recognize the importance of engaging in dialogue to understand and transcend those differences. . . .

When we initiate dialogue with the courage to recognize and accept others' differences, new horizons will open up before us. This has been the spirit with which I have engaged in dialogues with leading thinkers around the world.

We must learn from the differences that make each of us unique, and even make them a source of value creation.[11]

* * *

Revolution in the home is true social reform. Essentially, each child should be respected as an individual. Furthermore, it is important to stress mutual respect, social awareness, and the value of contributing to others welfare.[12]

University

Academic study and achievements are not merely to be tools for personal advancement. They should be utilized in the pursuit of happiness for others, and university study should be devoted to serving and contributing to the lives of those unable to pursue advanced learning themselves.[13]

* * *

The students are central to any university; they are its life. Universities originated from students wanting to further their studies coming together to form a learning community.

Why do we study? The greater and more profound our reason to study is, the brighter and higher will burn the flames of our desire to learn.[14]

Lifelong Learning

Life itself is a learning process, and learning as long as we live is the way to lead a fully human life.[15]

* * *

A university is not all there is to learning and education. Learning from and assimilating life can be even more valuable. Book learning acquires meaning only in the context of society. Otherwise it never actually becomes part of our flesh and blood. I, too, can say this from experience.[16]

Knowledge and Wisdom

Knowing how to apply the knowledge we have acquired— this is where wisdom comes in. We can accumulate all the knowledge we like, but without wisdom to guide us, it produces nothing of value. Memorized information alone always remains on the level of the conceptual.

Wisdom, in contrast, operates on the level of real life. It is a source of power for living, for surviving and coping. It is wisdom that leads to our success and happiness. Knowledge alone cannot produce happiness. Many people don't understand this, and remain under the illusion that knowledge is all that matters.[17]

* * *

Tsunesaburo Makiguchi insisted that the "aim of education is not to transfer knowledge; it is to guide the learning process, to put the responsibility for study into the students' own hands. It is not the piecemeal merchandizing of information; it is the provision of keys that will allow people to unlock the vault of knowledge on their own."[18] Of course, knowledge is important, but mastering the art of learning is most important of all. Once obtained, this key itself becomes a lifelong treasure.[19]

* * *

True intelligence is less a matter of knowing the "correct answer" than possessing the ability to ask pertinent questions.

Education for knowledge is a process of conveying a body of previously established facts. Of course, this is important in and of itself, but education for wisdom teaches the ability to explore and respond to the unknown. This is what education to foster the intellect should be.[20]

* * *

The ultimate goal of education and research is the good of humankind. Learning is the means, humanity is the end. We must never reverse these priorities. Knowledge acquired through the search for truth must be put to use for humanity. Computers are capable of storing information and using it to analyze problems. But only human beings can determine how such information will be used. In the end, only humans know how to teach others how to grow in wisdom and sensitivity.[21]

Education for Global Citizenship

Behind the discrimination, oppression, poverty, and human rights violations causing many of our problems, institutionalized violence extends everywhere from the home to international society. In relation to nature it takes the form of environmental pollution; in the human realm it causes infringements of human rights. True nonviolence is possible only if we overcome structural violence. Making people citizens of the world depends on education on peace, human rights, and environmental matters. These three mainstays are, in fact, integrated.[22]

In the coming era, we will require educational programs founded on a global outlook and global value criteria. They will need to stress developmental education that cultivates a caring attitude toward the poor and addresses global injustice. They should also emphasize human rights education forbidding discrimination and pursuing respect for human equality and dignity. Also, education that promotes respect for diversity so as to encourage lively intercultural exchange. Education that transcends the advantages of specific ethnic groups and nations and that works for the advantage of all humanity and the entire planet—in other words global citizenship education—is going to become increasingly important.[23]

Environmental Education

Environmental education, like peace education and human rights education, must be at the heart of a new vision of human education. By promoting the kind of education that empowers all people in their active quest for happiness and a better future, we can establish the foundations for a new era of hope in the twenty-first century.[24]

✳ ✳ ✳

Buddhism views the world as a web of relationality in which nothing can be completely disassociated from anything else. Moment by moment, the world is formed and shaped through this mutual relatedness. When we understand this and can sense in the depths of our being the fact that we live—that our existence is made possible—within this web of relatedness, we see clearly that there is no happiness that only we enjoy, no suffering that afflicts only others. In this sense, we ourselves—in the place where we are at this moment—become the starting point for a chain reaction of positive transformation. We are able not only to resolve our personal challenges but also to make a contribution to moving our immediate environment and even human society in a better direction. This palpable awareness of interdependence provides a framework or set of coordinates by which to reconsider the relationship between self and other and between ourselves and society as a whole. This is the approach that Buddhism urges us to adopt. Here, education is vital as it enables us to populate this field of coordinates with the actual experience of empathy felt when encountering the pain of others. Our perceptive capacities are honed by learning about the background and underlying causes of such issues as environmental degradation or human inequality, and this in turn clarifies and strengthens the system of ethical coordinates within which we strive to address these issues.[25]

Education About Human Rights

Only through learning can we open the spiritual windows of humanity, releasing people from the confines of ethnic or other group-based worldviews. Ethnic identity is deeply rooted in the human unconscious, and it is crucial that it be tempered through unremitting educational efforts that encourage a more open and universal sense of humanity.[26]

* * *

Educating people to be citizens of the world begins with cultivating respect, compassion, and empathy for others. I am certain that friendship and limitless trust in people can empower us to overcome socially disruptive discrimination and hatred.[27]

Science and Information Technology

Regrettably, even now in the twenty-first century, these stupid, senseless acts of discrimination still continue in many places around the world, causing countless individuals hardships and suffering. Since the dawn of recorded history, we know that humans have devoted themselves to endless technological progress. However, human consciousness does not have a corresponding maturity. In the twentieth century, in which each ensuing war used more advanced technological weap-onry, unprecedented numbers of lives were lost.

This reminds us that science and knowledge alone will never rid society of suffering. In this sense, the advancement of science and technology forces us to question the kind of education we need to perfect and elevate ourselves as human beings.[28]

Culture and Arts

A society that doesn't prize poetry or art would be an arid, des-olate world. It would be a society characterized by low regard for life and nature, dominated by egoism, and incapable of presenting anything but the most feeble resistance to evil. In this sense, we must reexamine and rediscover in education, too, the value and meaning of art in elevating human life.[29]

* * *

Human education must foster artistic and poetic sensibilities, which train and cultivate the human spirit, along with knowl-edge, reasoning powers, and a firm moral foundation. . . .

The arts and poetry are expressions of the vibrancy of human life and thus have the power to foster empathy and bring people together.[30]

* * *

I am convinced that restoring the spirit of poetry can restore education, thus becoming the driving force to enable stu-dents to win true happiness on their own.[31]

* * *

Discussing education without paying attention to culture is mere abstracting and misses the forest for the trees. . . . Some kind of cultural imprint is to be found in any and all aspects of education. Consequently, understanding culture profoundly is indispensable to grasping the true nature of education in all countries and among all peoples. . . .

The inclusive term *culture* embraces science, art, religion, philosophy, morality, and law as well as manners, mores, and systems. The products of all human activities, including education, are generated on the broad, multilevel ground called culture. If culture is figuratively the soil of symbiosis, all human activities are the plants and trees arising from it. The great tree of education that cultivates a rich humanity grows and thrives by drawing ample sustenance from the fertile cultural ground. The disposition inherent in a culture exerts an especially profound influence on the nature of education and its contents.[32]

Cultivating the Whole Person

In an ideal liberal arts education, before they specialize, students receive a broad background that helps them develop a comprehensive view of history and the world. In the present age of growing specialization and compartmentalization, it is increasingly important that we stand up for and maintain a commitment to the cultivation of the whole person.[33]

* * *

The important thing is never to lose sight of the purposes of research and knowledge as we strive to broaden and deepen both. Unfortunately, the more we subdivide and specialize, the more we tend to forget our points of origin. As this happens, learning often comes to exist as an end in itself. . . .

We need both a consolidated learning that integrates and evaluates segmented knowledge and an ethical philosophy to serve as a foundation. This need is one of the reasons for the recent reconsideration of the liberal arts and their approach to well-rounded education.[34]

APPENDIX
John Dewey and Tsunesaburo Makiguchi: Confluences of Thought and Action

June 2001, a paper originally prepared for the Center for Dewey Studies.

Although I never had direct, personal contact with Makiguchi (1871–1944), he was the teacher of my own teacher, Josei Toda (1900–58), and as such his philosophy and commitments have been a consistent presence in my life for more than half a century. During his long career as a primary school principal, he developed a unique theory of education that drew on his own teaching experience, his reading of contemporary educational theorists, including Dewey (1859–1952), and the Buddhism he embraced late in life.

During the final years of World War II, the Soka Kyoiku Gakkai (Value-Creating Education Society), the movement for educational, social, and religious reform founded by Makiguchi and Toda, was violently suppressed by Japan's militarist authorities.

Makiguchi and Toda were jailed and Makiguchi died in prison at age seventy-three. Toda, surviving the ordeal, rebuilt the organization as a populist movement, the Soka Gakkai (Value-Creating Society), based on the ideals of Buddhist humanism expounded by Makiguchi. My mentor's profound outrage against what he termed the "demonic nature of authority"—which had deprived Makiguchi of first his freedom, then his life—has been impressed indelibly on my being. It has driven my own determination to work for peace, for intercultural exchange and understanding, and for education.

Early Years in Meiji-Era (1868–1912) Japan

Most of the extant photographs of Makiguchi show an expression that can best be characterized as stern. Those who interacted with him, however, have described him as warm and compassionate. Makiguchi's empathy and support, particularly for the downtrodden, can probably be traced to the sufferings of his youth. The process by which Japan transformed itself, in the last decades of the nineteenth century, from a feudal, largely agrarian society into a modern industrial power was accompanied by large-scale dislocation and disruption. Niigata Prefecture, where Makiguchi was born in 1871, felt these changes deeply. The supplanting of traditional Japan Sea trading routes sent once prospering communities into decline. Amid extreme poverty, Makiguchi's father abandoned him at age three. His mother felt unable to care for him, and he was entrusted to relatives.

His efforts to continue his education were hampered by his adoptive family's poverty and the need to work to help support them. In 1885, at fourteen, he left home and moved to Japan's northernmost island of Hokkaido, where he found work as an errand boy in a police station. Recognizing his intellectual gifts, however, his supervisor supported Makiguchi's effort to attend a teachers college, from which he graduated in 1893 at twenty-two. The fact that he had not graduated from a prestigious national university was one impediment to the acceptance of his ideas within the Japanese educational establishment, which then—as now—placed foremost emphasis on formal pedigree.

It was during Makiguchi's days as a young teacher that Japan began pursuing in earnest a policy of national wealth and military strength—the path of imperial expansion. In the field of education, highest priority was likewise accorded to national aims, and all efforts were made to instill a blind, unquestioning patriotism.

For example, in October 1890, the Japanese government had issued the Imperial Rescript on Education in the name of Emperor Meiji. This document served as a powerful instrument of political indoctrination and remained in effect until the end of World War II. Certified copies of the rescript were distributed to every school throughout the nation, and it was ceremoniously read at all important school events.

Students were required to study and memorize the text for their moral education classes. This 315-character text defined Japan's unique national polity based on the historical bonds uniting its benevolent rulers and their loyal subjects. It also stated as an imperative that all Japanese subjects should cultivate virtues, central among them being loyalty and filial piety, for the greater glory of the imperial household. Makiguchi's assertion that the emperor should not demand this loyalty was one of the charges listed in the indictment against him at the time of his arrest in 1943.

The Geography of Human Life

In 1903, at thirty-two, Makiguchi published his thousand-page work, *Jinsei chirigaku* (The Geography of Human Life).

Makiguchi's interest in geography, in particular, the interaction between and impact of geographical features and human activities, finds a parallel in Dewey's own thought. As Dewey wrote in *The School and Society*:

> The unity of all the sciences is found in geography. The significance of geography is that it presents the earth as the enduring home of the occupations of man. The world without its relationship to human activity is less than a world.[1]

Makiguchi's *The Geography of Human Life* was published on the eve of the Russo-Japanese War, as a result of which Japan emerged on the world stage as a major power. The tenor of the times is symbolized by the fact that seven of Japan's most famous scholars from Tokyo Imperial University petitioned the government to take a hard-line stance against Russia, heightening public enthusiasm for war. In contrast, Makiguchi sought to promote the ideal of global citizens who, while rooted in the local community, would avoid the pitfalls of "narrow-minded nationalism." He also compared imperialism to thievery on a grand scale,[2] the outcome of national egotism.[3]

Makiguchi, in the same work, declared that "the freedom and rights of the individual are sacred and inviolable."[4] It is important to note that the Japanese emperor had been granted supreme sovereignty and power by the 1889 Meiji Constitution, in which he was described using these same words, "sacred and inviolable." To appropriate this language, intimately linked to the emperor, for this distinctly democratic usage, was, in the context of his time, nothing less than audacious.

While Makiguchi was critical of what he termed "narrow-minded nationalism," he was also skeptical of "vacuous, utopian globalism" devoid of actual content. He posited a three-layered scheme of identity or citizenship; education should instill a sense of belonging and commitment to the community, to the nation, and to the world.[5] Ultimately, he saw the welfare of the world as intimately linked with and necessary to individual well-being. Years later, in 1941, when Japanese society was fully under the sway of virulent ultranationalism, Makiguchi would return again to the theme of the interdependent connections between the individual and the life of the world:

> Unless the ultimate aim is established, intermediate aims cannot be fixed. Without perceiving the world, one cannot understand the nation. Unless the life of the nation is realized, individual livelihood cannot be secured. Therefore, if we are to achieve stability of individual livelihood in every household, that of the nation must first be established. Without the well-being of the world, that of a nation cannot be assured.[6]

Humanitarian Competition

Also in *The Geography of Human Life,* Makiguchi set forth his ideas about the path that human civilization had followed and the direction in which it should move. Influenced, like Dewey, by the Darwinian image of evolution, Makiguchi saw competition in its various forms as a driving force in history. Also like Dewey, Makiguchi never unquestioningly embraced the cult of progress but interrogated it from a variety of perspectives. He described the shifts over time in modes of national competition: from the military, to the political, to the economic—which he saw becoming, at the turn of the twentieth century, the predominant mode of competition.

Finally, moving from the descriptive to the predictive, he set out a vision of what he termed *humanitarian competition*—where he saw the future of his country and of humankind to lie. What Makiguchi described as humanitarian competition is not merely a locational or methodological shift in the competitive arena and modes. It represents a profound qualitative transformation in the very nature of competition, toward one that is based on a recognition of the interrelatedness and interdependence of human communities and that emphasizes the cooperative aspects of living.

He foresaw an age in which the power of character and the humane qualities of individuals and whole societies—manifested in the creative forces of their cultural achievements—would be a greater force than military prowess, political or economic domination. He envisaged a time when people and countries would compete—in the original sense of "seeking together"—to make the greatest contribution to human happiness and well-being.

He also saw humanitarian competition influencing and transforming other modes of competition.

The methods of humanitarian competition are not, of course, simple or unitary; all other forms of competition—military, political, economic—must be conducted within a humanitarian framework. In other words, the objective of states should not be merely the selfish pursuit of their own good but should be to enhance the lives of other peoples as well. We must choose those methods that profit ourselves while profiting others. We must learn to engage consciously in collective life.[7]

This echoes Dewey's call for "drawing out and composing into a harmonious whole the best, the most characteristic which each contributing race and people has to offer."[8]

Toward the end of this work, and without much elaboration, Makiguchi wrote that he saw the first signs of humanitarian competition emerging in the United States. At the same time, he clearly hoped that Japan would choose the path of humanitarian competition.

Makiguchi saw a special role for island nations, which, being connected by oceans to the rest of the world, tend to act as points of contact, interaction, and fusion among the world's cultures. He identified three island nations that he saw playing a pivotal role in the future of human civilization: Britain on the western edge of the Eurasian continent, Japan on the eastern flank, and the United States, which he considered an island nation writ large. Of these three, he saw the British Isles as already fulfilling the role of a cultural center; the United States was likewise destined, he felt, by location and by the multiple cultures it was embracing and absorbing, to become the future locus of human civilization. In Japan, he saw a similar potential and voiced his strong hope that this indeed would be the path Japan would choose to tread.

The Geography of Human Life closes with the hope that these three countries will make full use of their respective situations, propitious to the development of culture and the advancement of civilization, to engage in humanitarian competition for the benefit of the entire world.

Teaching Career and Educational Philosophy

In 1913, at age forty-two, Makiguchi was appointed principal of a primary school in Tokyo. For almost twenty years, he served in this capacity, assisting in the development of some of Tokyo's most outstanding public schools such as Shirogane and Taisho Primary Schools, at times even holding positions in two schools simultaneously.

As evidenced in his writing, Makiguchi was aware of Dewey's ideas and drew on them in his efforts to reform the Japanese educational system. In *The School and Society,* Dewey called for a Copernican revolution, by which the child becomes the center around which all educational endeavors must revolve.

Makiguchi likewise strove to make what we would now term *the best interests of the child* central to the theory and practice of education. He denounced the force-feeding of knowledge far removed from the realities of the child's everyday living. In its place, he called for education to have the happiness of children as its fundamental purpose. These sentiments can be sensed in the introduction to his 1930 work, *Soka kyoikugaku taikei* (The System of Value-Creating Pedagogy):

> I am driven by the intense desire to prevent the present deplorable situation—ten million of our children and students forced to endure the agonies of cut-throat competition, the difficulty of getting into good schools, the "examination hell" and the struggle for jobs after graduation—from afflicting the next generation. I therefore have no time to be concerned with the shift in vagaries of public opinion.[9]

Indeed, Makiguchi was relentless in his critique of those social structures and authorities that accepted or actively pro-

moted coercive and destructive modes of education. Makiguchi's views of education stood in sharp contrast to the
prevailing nationalist agenda with its focus on raising "little
national citizens." In *Pedagogy*, he asked: "What then is the
purpose of national education? Rather than devise complex
theoretical interpretations, it is better to start by looking to
the lovely child who sits on your knee and ask yourself: What
can I do to assure that this child will be able to lead the hap-
piest life possible?"[10] Makiguchi's focus of interest was never
the state but always people, individual human beings.

The System of Value-Creating Pedagogy, incidentally, offers the
one point of known, if indirect, contact between Makiguchi
and Dewey in the form of a shared friend, Japanese diplomat
and League of Nations under-secretary-general Inazo Nitobe
(1862–1933). Nitobe had encouraged Makiguchi's independent scholarship and wrote the foreword to *Pedagogy*, in which
he described Makiguchi's views on education as representing
a "major shift from the present idealistic approach to a genuine science of education."[11] And it was Nitobe who played host
to his longtime friend Dewey during his 1919 visit to Japan.

There was a strong preference in Japanese educational
circles for high-minded conceptual theories and contempt
for mere experience. In contrast, Makiguchi always stressed
an experience-centered approach. He strongly asserted the
importance of teachers assessing "cases of success and failure by analyzing their daily teaching experiences" as a basis
for the discovery of principles.[12] In other words, he believed
that principles should be extracted from experience and
not imposed on reality "from above." Makiguchi's own ideas
about education were derived directly from his experience as
a teacher and school principal. The four volumes of *The System
of Value-Creating Pedagogy* (twelve were initially planned) were
edited from the small mountain of notes he jotted on scraps

of paper that he kept with him always for that purpose, sometimes even pausing in midconversation to set down a thought.

What he had observed and experienced as a teacher were widespread suffering and the tragic waste of human potential. His first posting as a teacher had been to a remote, rural region of Japan, where he taught in the Japanese equivalent of a one-room schoolhouse. The children were poor, and the manners they brought from their impoverished homes were rough.

Makiguchi, however, was insistent: "They are all equally students. From the viewpoint of education, what difference could there be between them and other students? Even though they may be covered with dust or dirt, the brilliant light of life shines from their soiled clothes. Why does no one try to see this? The teacher is all that stands between them and the cruel discrimination of society."[13]

In 1920, Makiguchi was assigned as the principal of a primary school in one of Tokyo's poorest neighborhoods. With the end of World War I, the demand for wartime production that had boosted the Japanese economy collapsed, and the unskilled laborers who were the parents of Makiguchi's pupils were forced to compete for meager employment opportunities. Moved by the spectacle of dire need, Makiguchi prepared box lunches—which he paid for out of his own pocket—for children whose families could not afford them, and in order not to hurt their feelings, he left them in the janitors' room for children to take them freely. This predated by many years the establishment of a formal school lunch program in Japan.

Confrontation With Educational Authorities

In Makiguchi's time, it was customary for principals to visit the wealthy and influential families in the school district, a practice he consistently refused to follow. Makiguchi also refused to accept the prevailing custom of granting special treatment to the children of influential families and encouraged teachers working under him to do likewise. When wealthy parents sought special treatment for their children, Makiguchi flatly refused.

In 1919, this stance came to the attention of a leading local politician, who lobbied for Makiguchi's removal. Students, teachers, and parents all rallied to Makiguchi's defense and sought to have the transfer order stayed, even staging a three-day boycott of classes. Even after he had been transferred to another primary school, this same politician continued his campaign against Makiguchi. This time, Makiguchi made the educational authorities renovate a playground as a condition for accepting the transfer.

Because of these experiences, he insisted that it is crucial to create an inviolable realm for education, one protected from abuses of authority. To this end, he made a number of proposals in *The System of Value-Creating Pedagogy* and elsewhere. For example, he urged that an examination system be instituted for elementary school principals, to provide an objective, impartial basis for selection and to forestall selection of candidates with political or other connections. Also among Makiguchi's controversial proposals was a call to abolish the system of official inspection through which representatives of the central bureaucracy could directly interfere in the running of local schools.

Instead he advocated a democratic, participatory vision of education. He saw this as essential to assuring children's right to learn. He urged parents, and mothers especially, to become involved as active partners in their children's education. As mild as this may seem from the perspective of the present, it should be remembered that in Japan, until very recently, the standard expression for "parents" in relation to educational concerns has been *fukei* (literally, "fathers and elder brothers").

The Role of Teachers

What then is the concrete methodology of Makiguchi's value-creating education, and what roles does it suggest for teacher and learner? First, the emphasis shifts from education as the transmission of knowledge, a view that continues to predominate in Japan to this day, to education as the process of learning to learn. As Makiguchi put it:

> [Education] is not the piecemeal merchandising of information; it is the provision of keys that will allow people to unlock the vault of knowledge on their own. It does not consist in pilfering the intellectual property amassed by others through no additional effort of one's own; it would rather place people on their own path of discovery and invention.[14]

This quest for "discovery and invention" may be described as the learner's autonomous effort to discover and create value amidst the realities of life.

For teachers, this means several things. First, they must reassess their role as teachers.

> Teachers should come down from the throne where they are ensconced as the object of veneration to become public servants who offer guidance to those who seek to ascend the throne of learning. They should not be masters who offer themselves as paragons but partners in the discovery of new models.[15]

The role suggested here bears resemblance to Socrates's (c. 470–399 BCE) metaphor of the educator as midwife or, as drawn by Friedrich Wilhelm August Fröbel (1782–1852), gardener. The emphasis in Makiguchi's pedagogy is not on teaching so much as the work of carefully guiding the students' own process of learning.

Thus teachers must be diligent in their efforts to deepen their understanding of how learning occurs. To this end, Makiguchi, like Dewey, urged a commitment to an empirical method.

> Positivism says that we are to take the daily realities before us in education as our working knowledge, then wield the scrupulous scalpel of the scientist to dissect out educational theory; that is, to yield the constant truths at the root of educational practice. Only then will education embrace an integrally systematized body of knowledge. . . .[16]

This also requires continuous learning and personal growth on the part of educators. Makiguchi himself was already past fifty when he took up the study of English with the help of a textbook designed for junior high school students.

Another anecdote comes to us from Masataka Kubota, a teacher at the Nishimachi Primary School in Tokyo where Makiguchi was principal in 1920:

> Having worked for a number of principals, there was nobody as devoted to learning as Mr. Makiguchi. . . .
>
> The principal [Makiguchi] always had a newly published book in his hand, which he never monopolized, but always left for us to read, always inquiring after our impressions of the book.[17]

Philosophy of Value Creation

Central to Makiguchi's *The System of Value-Creating Pedagogy* was his theory of value. In his schema, he modified the neo-Kantian value system of truth, goodness, and beauty dominant in Japan at the time and reordered it as beauty, benefit (also translated as gain or utility), and good. He defined beauty as that which brings fulfillment to the aesthetic sensibility of the individual; benefit as that which advances the life of the individual in a holistic manner; good as that which contributes to the well-being of the larger human society.

While space does not permit a detailed analysis and comparison of Makiguchi's theory of value with Dewey's philosophy, a few points bear noting. Makiguchi removed "truth" from his list of values, seeing truth as essentially a matter of identification and correspondence; value, in contrast, is a measure of the subjective impact a thing or event has on our lives. While truth identifies an object's essential qualities or properties, value may be considered the measure of the relevance or impact an object or event bears on the individual. Makiguchi explains that

> value arises from the relationship between the evaluating subject and the object of evaluation. If either changes relative to the other, it is only obvious that the perceived value will change. The differences and shifts in ethical codes throughout history provide but one of the more outstanding proofs of the mutability of value.[18]

Dewey expresses a similar sense of historical and social contingency: "No longer will views generated in view of special situations be frozen into absolute standards and masquerade as eternal truths."[19] This aspect of Makiguchi's thought also parallels Dewey's critique of the centrality of epistemology in traditional philosophy and his focus on honing the tools of practical inquiry.

Following the suggestion of his young disciple, Josei Toda, Makiguchi coined the neologism *soka* for the creation (*sozo*) of value (*kachi*). The fundamental criterion for value, in Makiguchi's view, is whether something adds to or detracts from, advances or hinders, the human condition. This view resonates with what he found in Nichiren Buddhism, with its emphasis on manifesting one's innate human dignity amid the challenges of everyday life. The humanistic philosophy of Buddhism provided a firm and animating foundation for his theory of value.

The theory of value and value creation were central to the Soka Kyoiku Gakkai, which Makiguchi and Toda founded in 1930, with an initial membership of almost solely educators. At the time of its suppression by the authorities in 1943, the organization counted some three thousand members, from virtually all walks of life.

Through their various activities, members of the society sought to give form to Makiguchi's vision of education that would contribute to the lifelong happiness of learners. Firmly committed to the importance of "actual proof," these educators implemented the methods of value-creating education, recording and publicizing their results. As the organization's membership expanded and its activities shifted to a more purely religious focus, these same methods—of testing and proving—were applied to the realm of religious experience.

Experiential Learning for Global Citizenship

It was crucial, in both Dewey's and Makiguchi's view, to give children the opportunity to think and acquire experience in real-life settings.

This, of course, derived in Dewey's case from the philosophy of pragmatism, or as he preferred to term it, experimentalism. Contrary to the long-held view of experience as uncertain and anecdotal, Dewey reconceived experience as a fundamental, holistic function of life activity. Both Dewey and Makiguchi lamented the banishment of experience from the site of education. As Dewey describes it, the school was "so set apart, so isolated from the ordinary conditions and motives of life, . . . [it] is the one place in the world where it is most difficult to get experience—the mother of all discipline. . . ."[20] Makiguchi felt that the prevailing educational theories were "almost entirely unrelated to the realities of life."[21] He proposed a solution consonant in many ways with Dewey's own thinking:

> In-school education should be closely connected in practice with actual social life so that it can transform unconscious living into fully conscious participation in the life of society. Education integrated into the life of society will yield benefits of well-planned living, without the undesirable effect of mechanical uniformity, an inherent danger in standardized education.[22]

Dewey, linking school with everyday living, advocated the importance of guiding children to improve their social competence. In his words, a school should be a "genuine form of active community," "a miniature community, an embryonic society."[23] The essential aim of education implied here is the continuous, lifelong growth of an individual. This is brought about by acquiring experience, which evolves in depth and extensiveness from life in the home to that in school and finally to social life.

For his part, Makiguchi proposed a system in which students would attend class for a half day and spend the remaining half in "productive vocational activity," either assisting their parents' work, at a trade, or further specialization of study. Makiguchi wanted this system to be implemented for all students from the primary to the university level. According to him, it would have the following merits: it would encourage greater efficiency in teaching (which Makiguchi was convinced from his own experiences was possible); make more effective use of limited educational facilities by effectively doubling the number of students who could receive education at a school; alleviate the "examination hell" by which students competed for access to those facilities; and, most critical in Depression-era Japan, produce graduates with experience and capabilities that would enhance their prospects of finding meaningful work.[24]

Both Makiguchi and Dewey were, in their respective social contexts, pointing to a prevailing weakness in education, the impact of which was visible in all aspects of society. As it was conceived, school could not prepare students to think critically about social conditions or contribute constructively to their improvement. Moreover, the traditional educational methods remained distant from the empirical, scientific approach that was proving so effective in other fields of human endeavor. Dewey's Laboratory School and Makiguchi's proposals, such as that for half-day schooling, can be thought of as attempts to close this gap, as well as the gap between living and learning, which was of deep concern to both. In Makiguchi's words, we should not view "learning as a preparation for living, but enable people to learn in the process of living."[25]

For a child operating under her own initiative, learning may be described as innovative, investigative as well as creative. To kindle in all children an ever-burning passion for discovery, one that will lead them unfailingly to think for themselves, make their own decisions, and live out their lives accordingly—to do this is, in Makiguchi's view, to provide children the keys to the treasure house of knowledge.

Like Dewey, Makiguchi strove to realize a holistic approach to human development. For him, this meant enabling the student to engage in value creation, for which he set out six transformative indices. These are: from unconscious, emotional modes of living to a life of self-mastery, consciousness, and rationality; from a life of less to one of greater value creation; from self-centered to a social and altruistic mode of living; from dependent to independent modes of living in which one is capable of making principle-based judgment; from a life dominated by external influences to a life of autonomy; from a life under the sway of desires to self-reflective modes of living in which one is capable of integrating one's actions into a larger sense of purpose.

Ultimately, he cherished a vision of fostering people who could be described as true global citizens—individuals fully able to transcend self-seeking egotism and elevate their way of life to one linked to all of humanity.

Drawing inspiration from Makiguchi's thinking and from the Buddhist understanding of interdependence, I offered the following goals for education for global citizenship at a talk I gave at Teachers College, Columbia University, in June 1996 (see p. 3).

- ▸ The wisdom to perceive the interconnectedness of all life and living.
- ▸ The courage not to fear or deny difference but to respect and strive to understand people of different cultures and to grow from encounters with them.
- ▸ The compassion to maintain an imaginative empathy that reaches beyond one's immediate surroundings and extends to those suffering in distant places.

I am convinced that as we enter the twenty-first century, education that fosters these qualities is the most pressing imperative facing humankind.

In the Shadow of Totalitarianism

In 1939, the dark clouds of totalitarianism hung over the world. As Dewey warned in his *Freedom and Culture:*

> Democratic ends demand democratic methods for their realization. . . .
>
> Recourse to monistic, wholesale, absolutist procedures is a betrayal of human freedom no matter in what guise it presents itself.[26]

Japan was by this time fully caught up in the vortex of totalitarianism. Needless to say, neither the means nor the objectives were democratic.

The Japanese people had been manipulated into supporting the goals of imperial aggression and expansion in Asia under the guise of creating a "Greater East Asia Co-prosperity Sphere." This slogan, purporting pan-Asian coexistence and co-prosperity, was Japan's justification for replacing Western colonial imperatives and influence with its own.

In 1938, the National Mobilization Law stripped people of their civil rights and granted summary powers of government over national resources, both human and material. In the name of national defense, the entire nation was mobilized. In April 1939, the government enacted the Religious Organizations Law. This law empowered the government to disband any religious organization whose teachings or activities contradicted the "Imperial Way."

In 1941, the Peace Preservation Act of 1925 was revised, expanding its scope to prohibit—under penalty of life imprisonment or death—any acts that were seen as blasphemous of the emperor or of State Shinto, which asserted the emperor's divinity.

Makiguchi chose this time to launch a frontal critique of militarist fascism. At the time, most religions and religious organizations in Japan lent their support to State Shinto, which provided the philosophical and spiritual underpinnings for the prosecution of the war. Makiguchi, who had embraced Nichiren Buddhism in 1928, opposed this trampling underfoot of the freedoms of conscience and belief. Again and again, in writing and in speech, he criticized the government's stance. To the end, he refused to compromise his commitment to peace.

In 1941, the guiding principles of the Soka Kyoiku Gakkai were published in the first issue (July 21) of the organization's journal *Kachi Sozo* (Value Creation). Here, Makiguchi sought to express a balance between what he had long identified as the destructive aspects of unrestrained individualism and the totalitarian ethos that was sweeping Japan.

The Soka Kyoiku Gakkai shall be a gathering devoted neither to the individualism dictated by a myopic worldview that ignores the welfare of others nor the fallacious dictates of totalitarianism that divests the individual of his identity. Instead, it shall take as its highest honor to be a living testimony to a truly holistic way of life that is based on a correct and undistorted worldview.[27]

In the spring of 1942, *Kachi Sozo* was forced to cease publication at the order of the domestic security authorities.

Japan's military authorities were constantly vigilant against any sign of independence of opinion. They systematically undermined freedom of thought, conscience, and expression in their efforts to make the populace an obedient, sheeplike mass. Makiguchi expressed his firm conviction that "a single lion will triumph over a thousand sheep. A single person of courage can achieve greater things than a thousand cowards."[28]

In Makiguchi's theory of value, discussed earlier, good and evil are understood as relational. In many of his later writings, Makiguchi is harshly critical of what he termed "small good"—the passive avoidance of evil. He is insistent that "great good" could be realized only by confronting and challenging "great evil"—which he clearly identified as the actions and belief structures of militarist Japan.

As a result of these attitudes, Makiguchi was targeted as a "thought criminal," and his activities were subject to constant surveillance by the secret police.

Nevertheless, Makiguchi continued to organize small discussion meetings where he openly expressed his religious and moral convictions. According to his written indictment, he attended over the course of two wartime years more than 240 such meetings in different parts of Japan. In the presence of the police during these meetings, Makiguchi continued to criticize military fascism. Often his speech would be cut short by the police.

In November 1942, Makiguchi addressed the Fifth General Meeting of the Soka Kyoiku Gakkai. In that speech, he praised as "an incontrovertible truth" Dewey's assertion that our chosen way of living can be proven only within and through the act of actual living. The record of this meeting proved to be the last official publication of the Soka Kyoiku Gakkai.

In July 1943, Makiguchi and Toda were arrested by the dreaded special higher police. *Tokko Geppo* (Monthly Report of the Special Higher Police) reports the arrest of Makiguchi: "The thoughts and beliefs of [Soka Kyoiku Gakkai]–related persons centering on President Makiguchi manifest a number of subversive and seditious elements. Following secret investigations by the Police Agency as well as the Fukuoka Prefecture Special Higher Police Department, the agency on the seventh day of this month arrested and interrogated Tsunesaburo Makiguchi and five other persons for suspicion of blaspheming the dignity of the Imperial Grand Shrine and lèse majesté." Makiguchi was charged with expressing such opinions as: "The emperor is a common mortal"; "The emperor should not demand the people's loyalty"; and "There is no need to worship the Grand Shrine of Ise," a sacred site with close ties to the imperial household.[29]

Makiguchi was already seventy-two and spent the next year and four months, a total of five hundred days, in solitary confinement. Throughout, he refused to recant. Rather, he engaged in courageous dialogue with his interrogators and fellow prisoners, sharing with them the convictions for which he had been arrested. His stance remained, to the very end, one of a humanistic educator, committed to his own beliefs and opposed to the direction in which Japan was headed.

For example, under questioning, Makiguchi describes the ongoing war as a "national disaster"—not a "holy war" as it was officially characterized—that had been brought about by adherence to erroneous ideologies. He also repeated his assertion that the Japanese emperor is neither divine nor infallible.[30]

On November 18, 1944, he succumbed to the ravages of privation and brutal treatment, a martyr to the cause of human freedom and dignity.

Views of Religion

As mentioned above, Makiguchi was already fifty-seven when he embraced Nichiren Buddhism, an advanced age for an enthusiastic religious conversion. Dewey, having let lapse his ties to any specific church, sought to pursue religion as an impulse and experience ("the religious") outside the framework of any particular tradition. Makiguchi, in apparent contrast, adopted a lineage of Buddhism traceable to a specific teacher—in this case the thirteenth-century monk Nichiren (1222–1282). Despite this difference, their approach to religion and the function of religious faith are in fact deeply cognate.

First, both were adamant that religion must serve humanity; humanity does not exist to serve religion. Emblematic of this, Makiguchi rejected the neo-Kantian Wilhelm Windelband's (1848–1915) positing of the sacred as an independent category of value. Rather, he held that religion, to the degree it enhances the lives of individuals, generates the value of benefit or gain; and to the degree it contributes to the advancement

242 of society, creates the value of good. Beyond this, in Makigu-

of society, creates the value of good. Beyond this, in Makiguchi's view, religion had no purpose. This refusal to acknowledge "the sacred" as a self-sufficient value and his insistence
that religion has value only to the degree that it concretely
advances the human condition is deeply resonant with Dewey's rejection of the supernatural and his understanding of
"the religious" as that which can "unify interests and energies
now dispersed; it can direct action, generate the heat of emotion and the light of intelligence."[31]

Further, it should be noted that Makiguchi's embrace of
Nichiren Buddhism was the outcome of a highly conscious
process. His commitment to an empirical method of evaluation and choice making was so deep as to preclude anything
resembling blind faith or dogmatism.

This is illustrated by Makiguchi's own journey of faith. Born
to a Zen Buddhist family and having close Christian friends,
Makiguchi had gained exposure to a number of religious traditions. Although he felt that none of these faiths withstood
the test of scientific and philosophical inquiry, he refused to
dismiss religion per se as meaningless.

In 1928, as he was preparing the first volume of *Pedagogy,*
Makiguchi began to study the key Mahayana Buddhist text,
the Lotus Sutra. Here he was struck by a sense that the sutra,
and its interpretation by Nichiren, accorded fully with his own
rational principles.

This was not his first exposure to Nichiren. His foster family had practiced a form of Nichiren Buddhism, and he had
attended the lectures of Chigaku Tanaka (1861–1939), whose
interpretation of Nichiren's teachings was highly nationalistic and emperor centered. Makiguchi appears to have been
unimpressed by Tanaka's ideas, and they played no role in
shaping his own later reception of Nichiren's teachings.

When Makiguchi reencountered Nichiren Buddhism, this time in the form of the more humanist/pacifist reading of fellow educator Sokei Mitani (1878–1932), he found a system of religious thought that "revitalized" his theory of value.[32]

As a philosophy, Buddhism accords central importance to life. As Nichiren stated: "Life is the foremost of all treasures. It is expounded that even the treasures of the entire major world system cannot equal the value of one's body and life."[33] This clearly resonated with Makiguchi's own views: "The only value in the true sense is that of life itself. All other values arise solely within the context of interaction with life."[34] Both Buddhism and Makiguchi's philosophy contain a powerful critique of the prevailing militarist ideology that saw the lives of individual citizens and soldiers as subservient to—and expendable in—the overriding interests of the state.

From his writings, it is clear that Makiguchi saw the Soka Kyoiku Gakkai as a lay movement dedicated to realizing a "life of great good" through the practice of Nichiren Buddhism. As he is recorded saying during his police interrogation, his decision not to become a priest but to remain a lay practitioner stemmed from his desire not to be confined within a narrow sectarian interpretation of Buddhism.[35] Makiguchi clearly saw himself as returning to the core values of Buddhism, most notably a prioritization of human life and happiness, while at the same time developing ideational and organizational structures that could put these into practice in the twentieth century.

Specifically, the aspects of Nichiren Buddhism he found attractive were: (1) an emphasis on empirical experience and congruence with the scientific method; (2) the centrality of a universal law or principle (dharma) as the focus of faith rather than an anthropomorphic being or deity; and (3) an emphasis on social engagement and a stance of using religion's contribution to society as the measure of its validity.

Regarding the second aspect, the emphasis on the law over the person, Makiguchi felt that this was a mode of faith consonant with the historical trend toward constitutional democracy under an impartial rule of law, as opposed to rule by the despotic will of a single individual. "Rely on the law, not the person" is one of the famous injunctions of Buddhism, which Makiguchi repeated consistently. The law, in Buddhism, is the law of causality, of cause and effect.

This law, according to Makiguchi,

> is not confined to the physical present nor to the linear span of a single lifetime. It presides over humanity for time without end, in the boundless expanse of space and time, in the spiritual and the material realms. We live in its midst; we are inevitably subject to this law of causality.[36]

A Universal Law of Causality

Needless to say, the gulf between Makiguchi's principle-based view of religion and the dominant ideology in militarist Japan was vast. Starting in the 1920s, the government took an increasingly active interest in the religious beliefs and practices of its citizens. A series of ever-more stringent laws were passed restricting heterodox views and seeking to unify the spiritual resources of the nation under State Shinto. During the 1930s, several large sects were violently suppressed and their membership dispersed.

The structures of the militarist state were intimately intertwined with State Shinto, which forged from the indigenous animism of Japan an ideology of nationalism centered on the purity and "selection" of the Japanese race and the divinity of the emperor. Imperialist Japan not only enforced this belief system domestically but sought to forcibly export it. This disgusted Makiguchi who declared, "The arrogance of the Japanese people knows no bounds."[37]

To question any aspect of this ideology was to challenge the legitimacy of Japanese militarism, its policies, and their impact. The state became increasingly intolerant of dissent as the military position of Japan in the war became increasingly desperate. As stated, the Peace Preservation Act strictly outlawed any act or statement that could be construed as criticizing Japanese "unique national polity" (*kokutai*). It thus required enormous courage on Makiguchi's part to write, in the December 1941 Soka Kyoiku Gakkai periodical *Kachi Sozo*:

> We must strictly avoid following ideologies of uncertain origin that cannot be substantiated by actual proof—even if they may be the most time-honored tradition—and thereby sacrificing the precious lives of ourselves and others. In this sense, the question of [compulsory worship at] Shinto shrines must be rethought as a matter of great urgency.[38]

Again, Makiguchi returned to his belief in the all-pervasive Buddhist law of causality, rather than the caprices of individuals. He extended this outlook even to his understanding of Shakyamuni, the Buddha. Makiguchi is recorded as responding to his police interrogators as follows:

> Buddhism is not something invented or created by Shakyamuni (c. 560–c. 480 BCE). Without beginning

or end, it is a law governing and giving vitality to the
constant flow of all phenomena since time without
beginning. What is called Buddhism are simply acts
and practices that accord with this already existing law
or principle.[39]

To understand the nature of this law is to understand
Buddhism and at the same time Makiguchi's philosophy, a
philosophy of value creation that continues to inspire millions of people worldwide. In Makiguchi's view—and that of
Buddhism—the ultimate "law" is neither transcendent nor
anthropomorphic. It does not exist behind or above reality
but within it. As Nichiren explained in an exegesis on a sutra
passage: "'no worldly affairs of life or work are ever contrary to
the true reality.' A person of wisdom is not one who practices
Buddhism apart from worldly affairs."[40]

It was this commitment to reality, to experience, to people,
and to the work of finding real-life solutions to the problems
of living that sustained Makiguchi in his final confrontation
with the Japanese militarist state. These same elements have
been inherited and given concrete form in the global activities of the membership of the Soka Gakkai International.

In Conclusion

Although denied recognition during his lifetime, Makiguchi's
intellectual and spiritual legacy has had an important impact
in Japan and beyond. In the postwar years, the organization
Makiguchi founded was reconstituted as the Soka Gakkai by
his disciple, Josei Toda, growing into a Buddhist-based grassroots movement with membership in the millions. Today the
Soka Gakkai International has active members in some 163

[as of 2021, the number is 192] countries worldwide and is involved in peace education, environmental protection, and the promotion of international understanding through cultural exchange. Makiguchi's theories have begun to attract the serious interest of educators throughout the world.

It is also these same values—reality, experience, people— that form the most solid link between Makiguchi and the pragmatic philosophy of John Dewey. Inevitably, the course of their lives and careers, as well as the impact they exerted on their respective societies, diverge widely. But for just this reason, it is inspiring to learn from the lives of two men whose ideas and commitments developed along parallel paths united by a profound desire to contribute to human happiness, in particular the happiness of children.

Today, what our world requires most is a vast, collaborative effort by all those who share a commitment to empowering children and young people with the inner means for a lifetime of growth, happiness, and the creation of value. Toward this end, and inspired by the examples of these great men and others like them, I believe we must continue our efforts without cease.

Notes

Foreword

1. Shinichiro Yamamoto. "Pestalozzi the Great Educator (1949)," trans. Jason Goulah and Andrew Gebert, *Schools: Studies in Education* 17, no. 1 (Spring 2020): 150–52. Originally published in Japanese as "Dai kyōikuka Pesutarocchi" in the October 1949 issue of *Shōnen nihon* (Boys Japan). Shinichiro Yamamoto is a pen name of Daisaku Ikeda.
2. Daisaku Ikeda, Katsuji Saito, Takanori Endo, and Haruo Suda, *The Wisdom of the Lotus Sutra: A Discussion*, vol. 1 (Santa Monica, CA: World Tribune Press, 2000), 133.
3. Daisaku Ikeda, Katsuji Saito, Takanori Endo, and Haruo Suda, *Hokekyō no chie: Nijyūisseiki no shūkyō wo kataru* [The Wisdom of the Lotus Sutra: On Twenty-First Century Religion], vol. 4 (Tokyo, Japan: Seikyō Shimbun-sha, 1998), 181, 183. See Ikeda, Saito, Endo, and Suda, *The Wisdom of the Lotus Sutra*, vol. 4 (Santa Monica, CA: World Tribune Press, 2002), 139–40.
4. Mikhail Gorbachev and Daisaku Ikeda, *Moral Lessons of the Twentieth Century: Gorbachev and Ikeda on Buddhism and Communism* (New York: I. B. Tauris, 2005), 103.
5. See "Reviving Education" in this volume, p. 42.
6. See "Reviving Education" in this volume, p. 36; Jason Goulah, "Human Education: Daisaku Ikeda's Philosophy and Practice of *Ningen kyōiku*," *Schools: Studies in Education* 17, no. 1 (Spring 2020): 153–70; and Jason Goulah, "Introduction: Daisaku Ikeda, and Hope and Joy in Education" in *Hope and Joy in Education: Engaging Daisaku Ikeda Across Curriculum and Context*, ed. Isabel Nuñez and Jason Goulah (New York: Teachers College Press, 2021), xiii–xxxiv.
7. Goulah, "Introduction" in *Hope and Joy in Education*, xiii–xxxiv.

8. Daisaku Ikeda, "Waga kyoikusha ni okuru" [To My Educator Friends], in *Waga kyoikusha ni okuru: Ikeda Daisaku meiyo kaicho no shishin* [To My Educator Friends: Guiding Principles From Honorary President Daisaku Ikeda], ed. Soka Gakkai Education Department (Tokyo: Seikyo Shimbun-sha, 2015), 25.

9. Daisaku Ikeda, *My Recollections* (Santa Monica, CA: World Tribune Press, 1980), 55.

10. Goulah, "Introduction" in *Hope and Joy in Education*, xiii–xxxiv.

11. Daisaku Ikeda, *A Global Ethic of Coexistence: Toward a "Life-Sized" Paradigm for Our Age* (Tokyo: Soka Gakkai, 2003), 5.

12. Jason Goulah, "Daisaku Ikeda and the Soka Movement for Global Citizenship," *Asia Pacific Journal of Education* 40, no. 1, 35–48.

13. Goulah, "Introduction," in *Hope and Joy in Education*, xiii–xxxiv.

14. The modified Hepburn romanization style, the most widely used style for transliterating Japanese into English, includes a macron (¯) to indicate pronunciation for vowel combinations that form a long sound, such as the long *o* in *sōka*, *kyōiku*, *kyōsei*, Sōka Gakkai, Tsunesaburō, and Jōsei.

15. See "The Light of Learning" in this volume, p. xxi.

16. See "Building a Society That Serves the Essential Needs of Education" in this volume, p. 83.

Thoughts on Education for Global Citizenship

1. John Dewey, "Search for the Great Community," in *The Public and Its Problems: An Essay in Political Inquiry* (Chicago: Gateway Books, 1946), 154.

2. Henry David Thoreau, "The Village" in *Walden, The Selected Works of Thoreau,* ed. Walter Harding (Boston: Houghton Mifflin, 1975), 359.

3. *See* Alex Wayman and Hideko Wayman, trans., *The Lion's Roar of Queen Srimala: A Buddhist Scripture on the Tathagatagarbha Theory* (New York: Columbia University Press, 1974), 65.

4. Translated from Japanese. Takehisa Tsuji, ed., *Makiguchi Tsunesaburo shingen-shu* [An Anthology of Tsunesaburo Makiguchi's Works] (Tokyo: Daisanbunmei-sha, 1994), 40.

5. *See* Dewey, *The Public and Its Problems*, 213.

6. Translated from Japanese. Tsunesaburo Makiguchi, *Makiguchi Tsunesaburo zenshu* [The Complete Works of Tsunesaburo Makiguchi], vol. 7 (Tokyo: Daisanbunmei-sha, 1982), 183.

7. Translated from Japanese. Tsunesaburo Makiguchi, *Makiguchi Tsunesaburo zenshu* [The Complete Works of Tsunesaburo Makiguchi], vol. 6 (Tokyo: Daisanbunmei-sha, 1983), 289.

8. UN (United Nations). 1945. Charter of the United Nations, Article I. http://www.un.org/en/ sections/un-charter/chapter-i/index. html.

9. Translated from Japanese. Tsunesaburo Makiguchi, *Makiguchi Tsunesaburo zenshu* [The Complete Works of Tsunesaburo Makiguchi], vol. 8 (Tokyo: Daisanbunmei-sha, 1984), 365.

Realizing a Sustainable Future Through the Power of Education

1. Hazel Henderson and Daisaku Ikeda, *Planetary Citizenship* (Santa Monica, CA: Middleway Press, 2004), 138.

2. The Amaravati Sangha [Access to Insight], trans., *Karaniya Metta Sutta* [The Buddha's Words on Loving-kindness] (BCBS Edition, 2013). https://www.accesstoinsight.org/tipitaka/kn/khp/khp.9 .amar.html.

3. Aurelio Peccei and Daisaku Ikeda, *Before It Is Too Late* (London, I. B. Tauris, 2008), 125.

4. Private communication dated February 25, 2001.

5. Ben Okri, *Mental Fight: An Anthem for the Twenty-First Century* (London: Head of Zeus, 2021), 73–74.

Reviving Education: The Brilliance of the Inner Spirit

1. Simone Weil, "The Responsibility of Writers" in *The Simone Weil Reader,* ed. George A. Panichas (Mount Kisco, NY: Moyer Bell, 1977), 288.

2. See Hitoshi Nagai and Yoshiyuki Koizumi, *Naze hito wo koroshite wa naranainoka?* [Why Is It Wrong to Kill People?] (Tokyo: Kawade Shobo Shinsha, 1988).

3. Translated from Japanese. Albert A. Likhanov, *Wakamonotachi no kokuhaku* [The Confessions of Youth], trans. Ayako Iwahara (Tokyo: Shin-dokushoshin-sha, 1988), 161.

4. Norman Cousins, *Human Options* (New York: W. W. Norton, 1981), 40.

5. Johan Galtung and Daisaku Ikeda, *Choose Peace* (London: Pluto Press, 1995), 64.

6. Fyodor Dostoyevsky, *The House of the Dead*, trans. H. Sutherland Edwards (London: M. Dent & Sons, 1962), 55–56.

7. Jean-Jacques Rousseau, "Discourse on the Origin and Foundations of Inequality Among Men" in *Rousseau's Political Writings*, ed. Alan Ritter and Julia Conaway Bondanella, trans. Julia Conaway Bondanella (New York: W. W. Norton, 1988), 7.

8. Burton Watson, trans., *The Vimalakirti Sutra* (New York: Columbia University Press, 1997), 65.

9. Mahatma Gandhi, *All Men Are Brothers: Autobiographical Reflections* (New York: Continuum Publishing, 1990), 63.

10. Abraham H. Maslow, *Religions, Values, and Peak-Experiences* (New York: The Viking Press, 1970), 49.

11. Maslow, *Religions, Values, and Peak-Experiences*, 50–52.

12. *Kyoiku kihon ho* [Fundamental Law of Education]. Promulgated on March 31, 1947. The Fundamental Law was revised in 2006. http://www.mext.go.jp/b_menu/kihon/data/07080117.htm.

13. Translated from Japanese. Shugoro Yamamoto, *Nagai saka* [The Long Slope] (Tokyo: Shincho-sha, 1971), 17.

14. Translated from French. Albert Jacquard, *Petite philosophie à l'usage des non-philosophes* [A Modest Philosophy for Nonphilosophers] (n.p.: Calmann-Lévy, 1997), 18.

15. Leo Tolstoy, *Anna Karenina: A Novel in Eight Parts*, trans. Richard Pevear and Larissa Volokhonsky (New York: Viking-Penguin Putnam, 2000), 792.

16. Tolstoy, *Anna Karenina*, 794.

17. Tolstoy, *Anna Karenina*, 795.

18. Tolstoy, *Anna Karenina*, 796.

19. Tolstoy, *Anna Karenina*, 809.

20. Tolstoy, *Anna Karenina*, 813–14.

21. Tolstoy, *Anna Karenina*, 815.

Building a Society That Serves the Essential Needs of Education

1. Translated from Japanese. Taichi Yamada, "Ikitemiseru shikanai" [The Need to Demonstrate], *Chuo Koron*, September 1999.

2. *Kyoiku kihon ho* [Fundamental Law of Education]. Promulgated on March 31, 1947. The Fundamental Law was revised in 2006. http://www.mext.go.jp/b_menu/kihon/data/07080117.htm.

3. *Kyoiku chokugo* [Imperial Rescript on Education]. Promulgated on

October 30, 1890. Glorifying the values of loyalty and filial piety, the Imperial Rescript on Education was used as an absolute guiding principle and served as a powerful tool of ideological indoctrination. It remained in force until the end of World War II.

4. Founded in 1993, the Boston Research Center for the Twenty-First Century is located in Cambridge, Massachusetts. It was renamed the Ikeda Center for Peace, Learning, and Dialogue in 2009.

5. "Okinawa Charter on Global Information Society." https://www.mofa.go.jp/policy/economy/summit/2000/pdfs/charter.pdf.

6. Translated from Japanese. Tsunesaburo Makiguchi, *Makiguchi Tsunesaburo zenshu* [The Complete Works of Tsunesaburo Makiguchi], vol. 1 (Tokyo: Daisanbunmei-sha, 1987), 26.

7. Translated from Japanese. Nobukiyo Takahashi, *Mori ni asobu: Dorogame-san no sekai* [At Play in the Forest: The World of the Mud Turtle] (Tokyo: Asahi Shimbun-sha, 1992), 193–94.

8. Translated from Japanese. Tsunesaburo Makiguchi, *Makiguchi Tsunesaburo zenshu* [The Complete Works of Tsunesaburo Makiguchi], vol. 6 (Tokyo: Daisanbunmei-sha, 1983), 156..

9. Translated from Japanese. Tsunesaburo Makiguchi, *Makiguchi Tsunesaburo zenshu* [The Complete Works of Tsunesaburo Makiguchi], vol. 9 (Tokyo: Daisanbunmei-sha, 1988), 26.

10. Translated from Japanese. Tsunesaburo Makiguchi, *Makiguchi Tsunesaburo zenshu* [The Complete Works of Tsunesaburo Makiguchi], vol. 8 (Tokyo: Daisanbunmei-sha, 1984), 164–65.

11. William James, "The Moral Equivalent of War," speech given at Stanford University, 1906.

Humanity in Education

1. Victor Hugo, *Les Misérables*, trans. Lee Fahnestock and Norman MacAfee (New York: New American Library, 1987), 587.

2. Johann Wolfgang von Goethe, *Faust: Part One*, trans. Philip Wayne (London: Penguin Books, 1949), 46.

3. Translated from Japanese. Yukichi Fukuzawa, "Kyoiku no koto" [On Education] in *Fukuzawa Yukichi zenshu* [The Complete Works of Yukichi Fukuzawa], vol. 4 (Tokyo: Iwanami Shoten, 1959), 421.

4. *Fukuzawa Yukichi zenshu*, 4:422.

5. Henri Bergson, *The Creative Mind*, trans. Mabelle L. Andison (New York: Philosophical Library, 1946), 61.

6. See Alfred North Whitehead, *Essays in Science and Philosophy* (London: Rider, 1948), 126.

7. Plato, "Letters," trans. L. A. Post, in *The Collected Dialogues of Plato,* ed. Edith Hamilton and Huntington Cairns (New York: Princeton University Press, 1961), 1589.

8. Plato, "Meno," trans. W. K. C. Guthrie, in *The Collected Dialogues of Plato,* 363.

9. Translated from Japanese. Ogai Mori, "Teiken sensei" [Master Teiken] in *Ogai zenshu* [The Complete Works of Ogai], vol. 26 (Tokyo: Iwanami Shoten, 1973), 422–23.

The Flowering of Creative Life Force

1. Translated from Japanese. Charles Péguy, *Hangetsu techo* [Fortnightly Notebooks], trans. Imao Hirano (Tokyo : Akimori-sha, 1942).

Youthful Efforts Become a Lifetime Treasure

1. Jin Feng, *Deng Yingchao zhuan* [Chronicle of Deng Yingchao] (Beijing: People's Publishing House, 1993), 295.

2. Feng, *Deng Yingchao zhuan,* 295.

3. Deng Yingchao, *Deng Yingchao wenji* [The Writings of Deng Yingchao] (Beijing: People's Publishing House, 1994), 14–15.

4. Feng, *Deng Yingchao zhuan,* 78.

The University of the Twenty-First Century—
Cradle of Global Citizens

1. Thomasita Homan, "Alumna Plants Seeds for a Renewed Kenya," *Threshold,* (Spring 2003). http://www.mountosb.org/community/articles/maathai.html.

2. Judith Sutera, "Alumna Wins Nobel Peace Prize," *Threshold* (Winter 2004). http://www.mountosb.org/publications/thresholdwo4/peaceprize.html.

3. Translated from German. Wilhelm von Humboldt, *Werke* [Works], vol. 13, ed. Albert Leitzmann (Berlin: Walter de Gruyter, 1968), 261.

4. José Ortega y Gasset, *Mission of the University,* trans. Howard Lee Nostrand (London: Routledge & Kegan Paul, 1952), 47–48.

5. Ortega y Gasset, *Mission of the University*, 44.
6. Ortega y Gasset, *Mission of the University*, 44.
7. Ortega y Gasset, *Mission of the University*, 44.
8. Karl Jaspers, *The Idea of the University*, trans. H. A. T. Reiche and H. F. Vanderschmidt (London: Peter Owen, 1960), 21.
9. Jaspers, *Idea of the University*, 58.
10. Jaspers, *Idea of the University*, 145.
11. Jaspers, *Idea of the University*, 67.
12. John Dewey, *Democracy and Education* (Carbondale, IL: Southern Illinois University Press, 1985), 93.
13. John Dewey, *Problems of Men* (New York: Greenwood Press, 1968), 58.
14. Walt Whitman, *Democratic Vistas* (New York: Liberal Arts Press, 1949), 21.
15. Whitman, *Democratic Vistas*, 21.
16. Dewey, *Problems of Men*, 39.
17. Dewey, *Problems of Men*, 45.
18. Leo Tolstoy, *A Calendar of Wisdom*, trans. Peter Sekirin (New York: Scribner, 1997), 138.
19. Burton Watson, trans., *The Lotus Sutra and Its Opening and Closing Sutras* (Tokyo: Soka Gakkai, 2004), 70.
20. Ortega y Gasset, *Mission of the University*, 64.
21. Translated from French. Jules Michelet, *L'Étudiant* [The Student] (Paris: Calmann Lévy Éditeur, 1885), 226.

The Dawn of a Century of Human Education

1. Victor Hugo, *Les Misérables,* trans. Norman Denny (London: Penguin Books, 1982), 505.
2. Walt Whitman, "By Blue Ontario's Shore" in *Leaves of Grass* (London: Everyman's Library, 1968), 285.
3. See *Monbu jiho* [The Journal of the Ministry of Education], no. 880 (November 1950).

Soka Women's College—A Shining Citadel of Women's Education

1. Jean-Jacques Rousseau, *Confessions* (London: J. M. Dent and Sons, 1950), vol. 1, 80.
2. Simone Weil, *Attente de dieu* [Waiting for God] (Paris: La Colombe,

1950), 118. See http://simoneweil.net/attention.htm (January 30, 2004).

3. The Gosho Translation Committee, ed., *The Writings of Nichiren Daishonin*, vol. 2 (Tokyo: Soka Gakkai, 2006), 753.

4. Susan Quinn, *Marie Curie: A Life* (New York: Perseus Publishing, 1996), 83.

5. Eve Curie, *Madame Curie: A Biography*, trans. Vincent Sheean (Garden City, NY: Doubleday, 1937), 80.

6. Translated from Japanese. Marie-Irene Curie, *Haha to musume no tegami* [Correspondence Between Mother and Daughter], trans. Yuko Nishikawa (Kyoto: Jinbun Shoin, 1975), 108–9. Letter from Marie Curie to her daughter Irene, dated August 31, 1914.

7. Jane Addams, *Twenty Years at Hull-House, with Autobiographical Notes* (New York: MacMillan, 1937), 63.

Brief Thoughts

1. Nur Yalman and Daisaku Ikeda, *A Passage to Peace: Global Solutions from East and West* (New York: I. B. Tauris, 2009), 121–22.

2. Daisaku Ikeda, *The New Human Revolution,* vol. 15, Revised Edition (Santa Monica, CA: World Tribune Press, 2008), 237.

3. Daisaku Ikeda, "A New Humanism for the Coming Century" (Lecture, Rajiv Gandhi Institute for Contemporary Studies, New Delhi), October 21, 1997, https://www.daisakuikeda.org/sub/resources/works/lect/lect-09.html.

4. Daisaku Ikeda, "Humanity and the New Millennium: From Chaos to Cosmos." Published on January 26, 1998. https://www.sgi-usa.org/newsandevents/docs/peace1998.pdf

5. Ricardo Díez-Hochleitner and Daisaku Ikeda, *A Dialogue Between East and West: Looking to a Human Revolution* (New York: I.B. Tauris, 2008), 95.

6. Díez-Hochleitner and Ikeda, *A Dialogue Between East and West*, 87–88.

7. Daisaku Ikeda, *The New Human Revolution*, vol. 24 (Santa Monica, CA: World Tribune Press, 2013), 210–11.

8. Jim Garrison, Larry Hickman, and Daisaku Ikeda, *Living As Learning: John Dewey in the 21st Century* (Cambridge, MA: Dialogue Path Press, 2014), 84.

9. Translated from Japanese. Daisaku Ikeda, *Waga kyoikusha ni okuru*

[To My Educator Friends], ed. Soka Gakkai Education Department (Tokyo: Seikyo Shimbun-sha, 2015), 20–21.

10. Ikeda, *Waga kyoikusha ni okuru*, 59.

11. Ikeda, *Waga kyoikusha ni okuru*, 58.

12. Tu Weiming and Daisaku Ikeda, *New Horizons in Eastern Humanism: Buddhism, Confucianism and the Quest for Global Peace* (New York: I. B. Tauris, 2011), 9–10.

13. Ikeda, *New Human Revolution*, vol. 15, Revised Edition, 99.

14. Translated from Japanese. Daisaku Ikeda, *Ikeda Daisaku zenshu* [The Complete Works of Daisaku Ikeda], vol. 131 (Tokyo: Seikyo Shimbun-sha, 2006), 241–42.

15. Daisaku Ikeda, *The New Human Revolution*, vol. 23 (Santa Monica, CA: World Tribune Press, 2012), 86.

16. Hazel Henderson and Daisaku Ikeda, *Planetary Citizenship: Your Values, Beliefs, and Actions Can Shape a Sustainable World* (Santa Monica, CA: Middleway Press, 2004), 20.

17. Daisaku Ikeda, *Discussions on Youth: For the Leaders of the Future* (Santa Monica, CA: World Tribune Press, 2010), 366.

18. Translated from Japanese. Nichiren, *Nichiren Daishonin gosho zenshu* [The Complete Works of Nichiren Daishonin], ed. Nichiko Hori, (Tokyo: Soka Gakkai, 1952), 1547.

19. Weiming and Ikeda, *New Horizons in Eastern Humanism*, 21.

20. Ved Nanda and Daisaku Ikeda, *Our World to Make: Hinduism, Buddhism, and the Rise of Global Civil Society* (Cambridge, MA: Dialogue Path Press, 2015), 32–33.

21. René Simard, Guy Bourgeault, and Daisaku Ikeda, *On Being Human: Where Ethics, Medicine and Spirituality Converge* (Santa Monica, CA: Middleway Press, 2003), 198.

22. Díez-Hochleitner and Ikeda, *A Dialogue Between East and West*, 94–95.

23. M. S. Swaminathan and Daisaku Ikeda, *Green Revolution and Human Revolution* (New Delhi: Eternal Ganges Press, 2013), 79.

24. Daisaku Ikeda, "A Global Ethic of Coexistence: Toward a 'Life-Sized' Paradigm for Our Age." Published on January 26, 2003. https://www.daisakuikeda.org/assets/files/peace2003.pdf.

25. Daisaku Ikeda, "Universal Respect for Human Dignity: The Great Path to Peace." Published on January 26, 2016. https://www.daisakuikeda.org/assets/files/peaceproposal2016.pdf.

26. Daisaku Ikeda, "Toward the Third Millennium: The Challenge of

Global Citizenship," published on January 26, 1996, from *A Forum for Peace: Daisaku Ikeda's Proposals to the UN*, ed. Olivier Urbain (New York: I. B. Tauris, 2014), 252–53.

27. David Krieger and Daisaku Ikeda, *Choose Hope: Your Role in Waging Peace in the Nuclear Age* (Santa Monica, CA: Middleway Press, 2002), 177.

28. Vincent Harding and Daisaku Ikeda, *America Will Be! Conversations on Hope, Freedom, and Democracy* (Cambridge, MA: Dialogue Path Press, 2013), 206.

29. Garrison, Hickman, and Ikeda, *Living as Learning*, 210.

30. Harding and Ikeda, *America Will Be!*, 208–9.

31. Ronald A. Bosco, Joes Myerson, and Daisaku Ikeda, *Creating Waldens: An East-West Conversation on the American Renaissance* (Cambridge, MA: Dialogue Path Press, 2009), 145.

32. Gu Mingyuan and Daisaku Ikeda, "Humane Education, A Bridge to Peace (4)." *The Journal of Oriental Studies*, 22 (August 2012), 4–5. http://www.iop.or.jp/Documents/1222/3-35.pdf.

33. Weiming and Ikeda, *New Horizons in Eastern Humanism*, 127.

34. Harvey G. Cox and Daisaku Ikeda, *The Persistence of Religion: Comparative Perspectives on Modern Spirituality* (London & New York: I. B. Tauris, 2009), 85.

Appendix—John Dewey and Tsunesaburo Makiguchi: Confluences of Thought and Action

1. John Dewey, *The School and Society* (Chicago: The University of Chicago Press, 1990), 18.

2. Translated from Japanese. Tsunesaburo Makiguchi, *Makiguchi Tsunesaburo zenshu* [The Complete Works of Tsunesaburo Makiguchi], vol. 1 (Tokyo: Daisanbunmei-sha, 1983), 15.

3. Translated from Japanese. Tsunesaburo Makiguchi, *Makiguchi Tsunesaburo zenshu* [The Complete Works of Tsunesaburo Makiguchi], vol. 5 (Tokyo: Daisanbunmei-sha, 1982), 27.

4. Translated from Japanese. Tsunesaburo Makiguchi, *Makiguchi Tsunesaburo zenshu* [The Complete Works of Tsunesaburo Makiguchi], vol. 2 (Tokyo: Daisanbunmei-sha, 1981), 341.

5. *Makiguchi zenshu*, 1:15.

6. Translated from Japanese. Tsunesaburo Makiguchi, *Makiguchi Tsunesaburo zenshu* [The Complete Works of Tsunesaburo Makiguchi], vol. 10 (Tokyo: Daisanbunmei-sha, 1987), 7.

7. *Makiguchi zenshu*, 2:399.
8. John Dewey, *The Collected Works of John Dewey, 1882–1953, The Middle Works: 1899–1924*, vol. 10, ed. Jo Ann Boydston (Carbondale, IL: Southern Illinois University Press, 1980), 204.
9. *Makiguchi zenshu*, 5:8.
10. Translated from Japanese. Tsunesaburo Makiguchi, *Makiguchi Tsunesaburo zenshu* [The Complete Works of Tsunesaburo Makiguchi], vol. 4 (Tokyo: Daisanbunmei-sha, 1981), 27.
11. Translated from Japanese. Tsunesaburo Makiguchi, *Makiguchi Tsunesaburo zenshu* [The Complete Works of Tsunesaburo Makiguchi], vol. 1 (Tokyo: Tozai Tetsugaku Shoin, 1965), 397–98.
12. *Makiguchi zenshu*, 5:12.
13. Translated from Japanese. Tsunesaburo Makiguchi, *Makiguchi Tsunesaburo zenshu* [The Complete Works of Tsunesaburo Makiguchi)] vol. 7 (Tokyo: Daisanbunmei-sha, 1982), 183.
14. Translated from Japanese. Tsunesaburo Makiguchi, *Makiguchi Tsunesaburo zenshu* [The Complete Works of Tsunesaburo Makiguchi], vol. 6 (Tokyo: Daisanbunmei-sha, 1983), 285. Dayle M. Bethel, ed., *Education for Creative Living: Ideas and Proposals of Tsunesaburo Makiguchi*, trans. Alfred Birnbaum (Ames, IA: Iowa State University Press, 1989), 168.
15. *Makiguchi zenshu*, 6:289.
16. *Makiguchi zenshu*, 5:20. Bethel, *Education for Creative Living*, 7–8.
17. Genichiro Isonokami, *Makiguchi Tsunesaburo to Nitobe Inazo* [Tsunesaburo Makiguchi and Nitobe Inazo] (Tokyo: Regulus Library, Daisanbunmei-sha, 1993), 150.
18. *Makiguchi zenshu*, 5:236. Bethel, *Education for Creative Living*, 61.
19. John Dewey, "Search for the Great Community," in *The Public and Its Problems: An Essay in Political Inquiry* (Chicago: Gateway Books, 1946), 203.
20. Dewey, *School and Society*, 17.
21. Translated from Japanese. Tsunesaburo Makiguchi, *Makiguchi Tsunesaburo zenshu* [The Complete Works of Tsunesaburo Makiguchi], vol. 8 (Tokyo: Daisanbunmei-sha, 1984), 388.
22. *Makiguchi zenshu*, 6:199. Bethel, *Education for Creative Living*, 153.
23. Dewey, *School and Society*, 14, 18.
24. *Makiguchi zenshu*, 6:209.
25. *Makiguchi zenshu*, 6:212.
26. John Dewey, *Freedom and Culture* (New York: Prometheus Books, 1989), 13.

27. *Makiguchi zenshu,* 10:6.
28. Translated from Japanese. Takehisa Tsuji, ed., *Makiguchi Tsunesaburo shingen-shu* [An Anthology of Tsunesaburo Makiguchi's Works] (Tokyo: Daisanbunmei-sha, 1994), 26–27.
29. *Makiguchi zenshu,* 10:206. Japan. Special Higher Police, "Soka Kyoiku Gakkai Honbu Kankeisha no Chianijiho Ihan Jiken Kenkyo" [The Arrest of Persons Related With Soka Kyoiku Gakkai Headquarters for the Charge of Violating the Peace Preservation Law], *Tokko Geppo* [Monthly Report of the Special Higher Police] (July 1943), 127–28.
30. *Makiguchi zenshu,* 10:203. *Tokko Geppo,* 152, 156.
31. John Dewey, *A Common Faith* (New Haven, CT: Yale University Press, 1934), 52.
32. *Makiguchi zenshu,* 10:146. *Tokko Geppo,* 146.
33. The Gosho Translation Committee, ed., *The Writings of Nichiren Daishonin,* vol. 1 (Tokyo: Soka Gakkai, 2006), 1125.
34. *Makiguchi zenshu,* 5:232.
35. *Makiguchi zenshu,* 8:188. *Tokko Geppo,* 139–40.
36. *Makiguchi zenshu,* 8:63.
37. *Makiguchi zenshu,* 10:84.
38. *Makiguchi zenshu,* 10:26.
39. *Makiguchi zenshu,* 8:192. *Tokko Geppo,* 143–44.
40. *The Writings of Nichiren Daishonin,* 1:1121.

Index